bake it

150 favorite recipes from best-loved DK cookbooks

DK

Senior editor Carrie Love
Project art editor Polly Appleton

Project art editors Jaileen Kaur, Nehal Verma
Senior designer Nidhi Mehra
Project editor Radhika Haswani
Editorial assistant Becky Walsh
DTP designer Neeraj Bhatia
Illustrator Rachael Hare
Home economist Denise Smart
Pre-production senior producer Nikoleta Parasaki
Producer John Casey
Jacket designer Elle Ward
Jacket co-ordinator Issy Walsh
Project picture researcher Sakshi Saluja
Delhi team head Malavika Talukder
Managing editors Penny Smith, Monica Saigal
Managing art editors Mabel Chan, Romi Chakraborty
Creative director Helen Senior
Publishing director Sarah Larter

First American Edition, 2019
Published in the United States by DK Publishing
1450 Broadway, Suite 801, New York, New York 10018

Material used in this book was previously published in:
The Cook's Book (2005),
The Children's Baking Book (2009),
The Illustrated Step-by-step Cook (2010),
Step-by-Step Baking (2011),
Get Started Baking (2013),
Step-by-Step Cake Decorating (2013),
Kids' Birthday Cakes Step by Step (2014),
Desserts (2015),
Eat Your Greens (2016),
Cooking Step by Step (2018)

Copyright © 2019 Dorling Kindersley Limited
DK, a Division of Penguin Random House LLC
19 20 21 22 23 10 9 8 7 6 5 4 3 2 1
001–314399–Oct/2019

A catalog record for this book is available from the Library of Congress.
ISBN 978-1-4654-8614-1

DK books are available at special discounts when purchased in bulk for sales promotions, premiums, fund-raising, or educational use. For details, contact: DK Publishing Special Markets, 1450 Broadway, Suite 801, New York, New York 10018 SpecialSales@dk.com

Printed and bound in China

All images © Dorling Kindersley Limited
For further information see: www.dkimages.com

A WORLD OF IDEAS:
SEE ALL THERE IS TO KNOW

www.dk.com

Contents

Creative cakes, cupcakes, and muffins

No-bakes

Kitchen rules

Baking is meant to be fun and a little bit messy, but you still need to keep safety and cleanliness in mind. Follow instructions carefully, gather everything together, and read through these rules and tips before you begin.

Ingredients

- Make sure you have all your ingredients laid out before you start to make a recipe. You'll probably have most ingredients in your kitchen already, but some you will need to buy.

- Always use the type of flour specified in a recipe—bread, all-purpose, or self-rising.

- Use medium-sized eggs unless stated otherwise.

Preheating the oven

Follow the temperature instructions within each recipe.

Special equipment

Keep an eye out for recipes that require special equipment. Buy or borrow items in advance if you don't own them.

Weights and measurements

Carefully weigh the ingredients before you start a recipe. Use measuring spoons, weighing scales, and a liquid measuring cup as necessary. Below are the abbreviations and full names for the measurements used in this book.

Metric	US measures	Spoon measures
g = gram	oz = ounce	tsp = teaspoon
ml = milliliter	lb = pound	tbsp = tablespoon

Level rating

Each recipe has a level rating to let you know how easy it will be to make.

 Super simple

 Nice and easy

 A bit tricky

 Super skilled

How long?

This tells you how many minutes and hours a recipe will take to prepare, bake, chill, or freeze. Remember though that preparation times may take a little longer if it's the first time you're making a recipe.

How many?

This lists the amount of portions a recipe makes. Remember to be treat wise and don't go overboard by eating more than one portion.

Top tip

You'll find extra bits of advice in the Top tips throughout the book.

Kitchen safety

Be very careful...

- Around hot ovens and gas or electric stoves, making sure you know whether the oven or stove is on and protecting your hands when touching or lifting anything hot from or into it. Oven mitts are your friend here!

- Handling hot liquids or hot pans, watching carefully for spills, and protecting your hands (with oven mitts or a dish towel) when moving or holding hot items. Tell an adult immediately if you get a burn.

- Handling anything sharp, such as knives or a grater.

- Using power tools, such as blenders, food processors, mixers, and microwaves. Check if they're on, and don't put your hands near the moving parts until you have switched the power off at the outlet.

IF IN DOUBT, ask an **ADULT** to help, especially when you're unsure about anything.

TRY THIS

Look for these variation suggestion boxes. You can sometimes alter the ingredients to create a slightly different version of a recipe.

Kitchen hygiene

When you're in the kitchen, follow these important rules to keep the germs in check.

- Always wash your hands before you start any recipe.

- Wash all fruits and vegetables.

- Use separate cutting boards for meat and vegetables. Use hot, soapy water to clean the boards after using them.

- Store raw and cooked food separately.

- Keep meat in the fridge until you need it and always make sure to cook it properly.

- Wash your hands after handling raw eggs or raw meat.

- Always check the use-by date on all ingredients.

- Keep your cooking area clean and have a cloth handy to mop up any spills.

Getting started

1

Read a recipe all the way through before you start.

2

Wash your hands, put on an apron, and tie back your hair.

3

Make sure you have all the ingredients and equipment on hand before you begin cooking.

Equipment

Here is a handy guide for the baking equipment used throughout this book. Always follow the guidelines in the recipes for a particular size pan, sheet, or dish, since the ingredients may not fit otherwise.

Kitchen scissors Paintbrushes Peelers Garlic press

Wooden spoons | Whisk | Pastry brush | Large metal spoon | Serrated knife | Sharp knife | Pizza cutter | Table knife | Fork | Spoons | Sugar thermometer

Pizza pan

Square cake pan

Baking sheets and pans

Paper cupcake liners

Loaf pan

12-hole cupcake pan

Round cake pan

Paper muffin liners

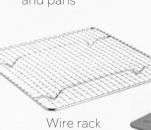 

Wire rack

Mini cake pan about 2½ x 1in (6.5 x 2.5cm)

Nonstick muffin pan

Cutting boards

Large bowl | Metal bowl | Glass bowls | Small bowls | Milk pan

Measuring
spoons

Measuring cups

Glass pitchers

Food
processor

Blender

Electric
mixer

Injector

Plunger cutters

Piping bag
and nozzles

Ramekin

Lemon juicer

Cookie cutters

Pastry cutter

Sieve

Slotted
spoon

Palette
knife

Spatula

Plastic
spatula

Ice cream
scoop

Fluted
wheel

Zester

Measuring cup

Rolling pin

Parchment
paper

Plastic
container

Baking beans

Colander

Spray bottle

Grater

Foil

Plastic
wrap

Skewers

4in (10cm) loose-
bottomed pie pan

Baking dish

Pie dish

Metal flan dish

Frosting smoother

Frying pan

A selection of saucepans,
including a heavy-bottomed one

Lazy Susan

Frosting
scrapers

Baking techniques

To get cakes to rise, make light meringue, and perfect your pastry and cookies, there are certain techniques in baking that you'll need to master. Once you know what's what you'll be a baking expert!

Fold

1 Use a spatula to gently mix while keeping the air in the mixture.

2 Go around the edge of the bowl and then "cut" across the middle, lifting as you go.

Sift

Shaking flour or confectioners' sugar through a sieve gets rid of lumps and adds air.

Separate an egg

1 To break the shell, tap the egg on the side of the bowl and open it up.

2 Transfer the yolk from one shell to the other; put the yolk in another bowl.

Beat egg whites

1 In a spotlessly clean bowl, mix a lot of air into the egg whites, using an electric mixer.

2 The egg whites should be stiff. If you beat them too much, they will collapse, as shown here.

Knead

1 Use the heel of your hand to push the dough away from you.

2 Fold the squashed end of dough over and turn the whole piece of dough around.

3 Repeat the squashing, folding, and turning motions until the dough is silky soft and smooth. Now the dough is ready to proof (get bigger).

Punch down

To "punch down" the dough, lightly punch it. This knocks out any large air bubbles.

Roll out

On a floured surface, roll a rolling pin over the dough to flatten it out.

Cream

1 When mixing butter and sugar together, use butter that's been left to soften at room temperature. Cut the butter into pieces first.

2 Using an electric mixer or a wooden spoon, beat the butter and sugar together until it's paler in color, light, and fluffy.

Beat

Make a smooth, airy mixture by stirring quickly with a wooden spoon.

Rub in

1 Many recipes mix fat (diced butter or lard) and flour using this method.

2 Using your fingertips, pick up the mixture, break up the lumps, and let it fall.

3 Keep rubbing your thumb along your fingertips. To check that you've gotten rid of lumps, shake the bowl. Any lumps will pop up to the surface.

Shortcrust pastry

This pastry is used to line savory and sweet tarts and pies, and it doesn't puff up on baking. For light pastry, the key is to keep everything cool, including your hands, and not to overwork the dough.

1 It is important to use only your fingertips when rubbing the butter into the flour, as this minimizes contact with body heat, which will melt the butter and make the pastry heavy and greasy.

2 Mix in enough cold water to bind the dough together. Too much water will make the pastry steam on baking, which will make it fragile and shrink back. The dough should be soft, but not sticky, once fully mixed.

3 Shape the dough into a ball without overworking it, which could make the pastry greasy and tough. Shortcrust pastry must be chilled in the fridge for at least 30 minutes before shaping it into a pan to bake.

Grease a pan

Use baking parchment to spread a thin layer of butter all over the inside of the pan.

Line a pan

1 Draw around the pan. Cut out the shape, leaving enough extra parchment paper to cover the sides of the pan.

2 Position the paper in the pan so it covers the bottom and the sides. Cut off the overhang.

Choux pastry

Choux pastry is a very light and airy pastry that is used for making profiteroles. By beating enough air into the soft, doughy mixture you will guarantee a crisp and light pastry that will rise beautifully as it bakes.

1 The traditional technique for beating flour into melted butter and water is called "shooting" the flour. Beat the mixture vigorously, but stop when it forms a ball of soft dough that comes away from the sides of the pan.

2 Using a wooden spoon, beat the eggs into the mixture a little at a time. Adding the eggs one at a time makes it easier to mix them in and with each beating you add more air. The dough should now be soft enough to pipe.

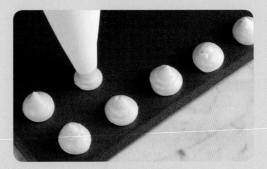

3 Fit a piping bag with a plain nozzle and fill it with the dough. With one hand at the top of your piping bag and one at the bottom, squeeze the dough out from the top into even rounds, leaving space in between each one.

Frosting and icing

Buttercream frosting is the perfect covering for cakes and cupcakes, royal icing is great for piping work, as it hardens quickly, and traditional royal icing is ideal for attaching cake decorations. Here are the best methods for making them.

Vanilla buttercream frosting

Ingredients

20 tbsp unsalted butter
2 tsp vanilla extract
7 cups confectioners' sugar
coloring paste (optional)

1 Cream the butter and vanilla together with an electric mixer. Add the confectioners' sugar, beating well. Beat in 1–2 teaspoons of hot water. Mix until the frosting is light and fluffy.

2 Transfer to a bowl and add coloring paste, a little at a time, until you get the right color.

Royal icing for piping

Ingredients

3 large egg whites
1 tsp lemon juice, plus extra if needed
7 cups confectioners' sugar, sifted
coloring paste (optional)

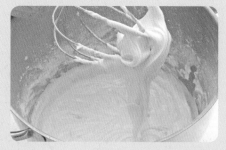

1 Beat the egg whites in a large bowl. Stir in the lemon juice. Gradually add the sugar.

2 Continue to beat until the icing has a smooth, toothpaste-like consistency.

Traditional royal icing

Ingredients

3 large egg whites
7 cups confectioners' sugar, sifted, plus extra if needed
1 tsp lemon juice
2 tsp glycerine

1 Beat the egg whites in a large bowl until they are foamy. Add the sugar a spoonful at a time.

2 Stir in the lemon juice and glycerine, and beat until stiff, thick, and peaks begin to form.

Piping

Piping icing onto a cake takes a steady hand, so don't worry if you don't master it right away. It's all about getting lots of practice. Here are tips for filling a piping bag and applying the icing to a baked cake.

Filling a piping bag

1 Fit the nozzle to the piping bag and place it upright in a tall glass. Spoon in the buttercream frosting.

2 Remove the bag from the glass and squeeze the icing toward the nozzle. Lay the bag on a surface and press toward the nozzle, using a scraper, if desired.

3 Twist the bag at the top, to make sure that the frosting is tightly sealed in. Hold the bag in one hand and steady the nozzle with your other hand. Squeeze the top of the bag (just below the twist) to get the buttercream to come out.

Basic royal icing piping

1 Fill the piping bag with royal icing. Hold the bag in your right hand (or left, if you are left-handed), between your thumb and first two fingers. Hold the bag steady with your other hand. When the nozzle touches the surface of the cake, gently squeeze the icing out.

2 Use even pressure, since too little pressure will produce scrawny lines, while too much will make piping difficult to control. Let the icing catch the surface and then gently lift the nozzle away from the surface, letting the icing fall. At the end of the line, stop the pressure and lift the nozzle away.

Filling and layering cakes

Impressive cakes often have several layers. Follow the steps below for layering a cake with frosting to build several levels. Before you frost a cake, do a crumb-coat layer first, since this prevents pieces from coming off when you frost the cake.

Testing a cake is baked

Insert a skewer into the middle of the cake. If it comes out clean, the cake is baked.

Leveling a cake

Carefully remove the dome from the top of the cake using a serrated knife.

Layering and crumb coating a cake

1 Put the board on a lazy Susan, dot with a dollop of frosting, and center the bottom layer on top, leveled-side up. Pipe frosting around the edge.

2 Using a spoon, put a large dollop of frosting in the center and spread to the edges with a palette knife, until smooth.

3 Put the next layer on, leveled-side down. To build the cake higher, repeat, with the leveled sides facing each other.

4 To crumb coat the cake, start at the top and swirl the frosting over the surface as you turn it around on the lazy Susan.

5 Spread the frosting around the sides until evenly covered. A few crumbs may be embedded in the frosting; this is normal.

6 Refrigerate or allow to dry—this can take up to two hours. Add the final layer of frosting.

Frosting a cake

This method works best of all with buttercream frosting, although you can use ganache or whipped cream instead. Using a palette knife and scraper, smooth your cake to an absolutely perfect finish.

1 With the cake on the lazy Susan, put a large dollop of buttercream frosting onto the center of the cake.

2 Using a palette knife, swirl and smooth the frosting, spreading it outward and over the sides as you go.

3 Turn the cake as you spread the frosting down and around the sides, to cover it evenly. When smooth, let the cake set for 10 minutes, and then repeat.

4 Put the blade of a palette knife in a bowl of boiling water. When it is hot, dry it, and run it around the sides, turning the cake around with the flat surface of the knife against the frosting. Repeat until the frosting is smooth.

5 Make the top smooth with a hot knife, turning the cake with the flat surface of the knife against the frosting. Move from one side of the cake to the other. Allow the cake to set for 15 minutes.

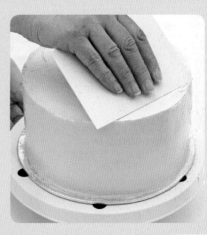

6 Use a scraper to smooth the frosting all the way around the cake.

Piping cupcakes

Put a jam or frosting filling into your cupcakes. Then, for a professional-looking finish, pipe buttercream frosting into a swirl. Alternatively, try out different nozzles for stars, shells, or a variety of effects and textures. To finish, sprinkle your favorite toppings over the piped frosting.

1 If you have thin, smooth frosting or jam, you can use a plain round nozzle (shown above) or an injector nozzle on a piping bag. Attach the nozzle, load the bag with filling, and push it into the center of the cupcake. Gently press on the bag until the frosting fills the hole you've just made.

2 To frost the top of the cupcake, hold the nozzle ½in (1cm) straight above the cupcake and pipe from the outside edge inward in a spiral. Apply pressure so that an even amount comes out.

3 Build several layers of frosting in a spiral movement, making each layer slightly smaller as you go.

4 Release the pressure to end the spiral at the center of the cupcake. Decorate with sprinkles or edible glitter.

Covering a cake

Add an outer layer of rolled-out fondant or marzipan to cakes for an extra-special finish. Flatten out the air bubbles as you cover a cake with this clever technique using a smoother. The thickness of the fondant or marzipan should only ever be ⅛-¼in (4–5mm), so it doesn't overpower the flavors in the cake.

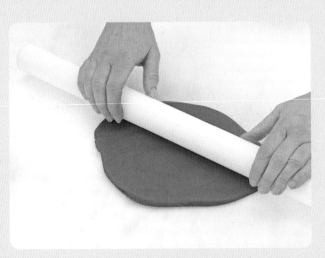

1 Dust a surface with confectioners' sugar. Knead and roll the fondant or marzipan into a circle that can cover the cake with 2in (5cm) extra overhang.

2 Unroll the fondant or marzipan sheet onto the cake and smooth it across the top with a smoother, easing it down with your hands.

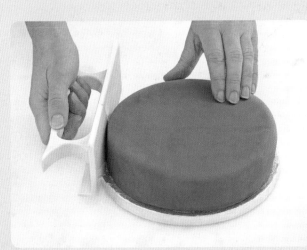

TRY THIS

For mini cakes, the fondant should be ¹⁄₁₆–⅛in (2–3mm) thick. For cupcakes, cut out circles of fondant to sit on top of the cupcakes.

3 Trim off the excess fondant or marzipan. Press the smoother evenly over the top of the cake and then run it down and around the sides of the cake, until perfectly smooth. To get a sharp edge at the top of the cake, you can use two smoothers at the same time, one on the top and the other on the sides, pressing them together at the edge.

Making meringues

Meringues are made by beating lots of air into egg whites, then beating in sugar. The mixture is then shaped and baked slowly on low heat so that the moisture in the mixture evaporates, leaving you with crisp meringues that are light as air.

Use a clean bowl, with no grease.

Scrape the sides of the bowl with a spatula.

1 For a light and crisp meringue, you must beat the egg whites vigorously using an electric mixer. This stretches the protein in the egg whites, which helps to incorporate air into the mix and, as a result, increases the volume in the egg whites.

2 Using an electric mixer, beat in a spoonful of sugar at a time; any quicker and you may deflate the mixture. The beaten egg whites will become smoother and glossier with every addition of sugar.

Beat until peaks form.

Top tip

The egg whites and bowl must be free from any grease or egg yolk, otherwise they won't beat into stiff peaks.

3 Make sure to dissolve the sugar into the egg whites by beating very well after each addition. The mixture will no longer feel grainy when the sugar has fully dissolved.

Melting chocolate

Whether you want to wrap a cake in chocolate, use molds to create chocolate decorations, or make decorative curls, you must melt and temper chocolate. Tempering chocolate improves its consistency before you use it and gives a hard and glossy finish once it cools down.

Level rating

How long?
10 mins prep,
10 mins cooking

How many?
1lb 2oz (500g), enough to cover
a cake or fill 3 large molds

Ingredients

1lb 2oz (500g) good-quality
milk, dark, or white chocolate

Special equipment
sugar thermometer

In a microwave

1 Break the chocolate into squares, put the squares in a microwavable bowl, and heat on full power for 30 seconds. Stir, and heat again in 15-second bursts, until the chocolate is smooth and melted.

2 Test the temperature and continue to heat in short bursts, until it reaches 113°F (45°C). Let it cool until the temperature reaches 80°F (27°C), stirring frequently. The chocolate should remain at this temperature as you use it—warm it a little if the temperature drops too low.

On a stovetop

1 Melt chocolate pieces in a heatproof bowl over a pan of simmering water. The bowl should not touch the water.

2 Stir occasionally to distribute the heat. Heat until the sugar thermometer measures 113°F (45°C).

3 Remove from the heat and let the chocolate cool until the temperature reaches 80°F (27°C), stirring frequently.

CREATIVE CAKES, CUPCAKES, AND MUFFINS

Whip up divinely soft sponge cakes and pretty cupcakes for all your friends. Treat times will never be the same again with these irresistible loaves, moist muffins, and fruity cheesecakes!

Blueberry muffins

These light and fluffy muffins are topped with zingy lemon juice for an extra burst of flavor. They are best served warm.

Ingredients

4 tbsp unsalted butter

1⅓ cups all-purpose flour

1 tbsp baking powder

pinch of salt

¾ cup granulated sugar

1 large egg

finely grated zest and juice of 1 lemon

1 tsp vanilla extract

1 cup milk

8oz (225g) blueberries

Special equipment

12-hole muffin pan

12 paper liners

1 Preheat the oven to 425°F (220°C). Melt the butter in a pan over medium-low heat.

2 Sift the flour, baking powder, and salt into a bowl. Set two tablespoons of sugar aside and stir the rest into the flour. Make a well in the center.

3 In a separate bowl, beat the egg lightly until just broken down and mixed together. Add the melted butter, lemon zest, vanilla, and milk. Beat until foamy.

4 Pour the egg mixture into the flour. Then gradually stir it into the dry ingredients to make a smooth batter.

5 Gently fold in all the blueberries. Do not overmix or the muffins will be tough.

6 Place the paper liners in the muffin pan. Spoon in the batter; filling each liner three-quarters full.

8 In a small bowl, stir the reserved sugar with the lemon juice until the sugar dissolves.

7 Bake for 15–20 minutes. Let the muffins cool slightly, then transfer them to a wire rack.

9 While the muffins are still warm, dip the top of each into the sugar and lemon mixture.

Top tip

The muffins will keep in an airtight container for two days.

10 Set the muffins upright back on the wire rack and brush with any remaining glaze.

Pizza muffins

Cheese and pepperoni give these savory muffins a delicious flavor. Instead of having something sweet, try nibbling on these when you're hungry.

Level rating

How long?   15 mins prep,
                 25 mins baking

How many?   8–10

Ingredients

oil, for greasing

1½ cups all-purpose flour

1 tsp baking powder

1 tsp dried oregano

8 tbsp butter, melted

1 cup + 2 tbsp milk

2 large eggs

2 tbsp pizza sauce, plus extra
   for dipping

4oz (115g) mixed Cheddar
   and mozzarella cheese, grated

5½oz (150g) mini pepperoni, sliced

Special equipment

2 x 6-hole or 1 x 12-hole muffin pan

TRY THIS

To make a veggie version, replace the same quantity of mini pepperoni with pitted black olives, cut lengthwise.

1 Preheat the oven to 375°F (190°C) and grease a muffin pan with oil.

2 Mix the flour, baking powder, and oregano in a bowl. Mix the butter, milk, eggs, and pizza sauce in a liquid measuring cup.

3 Pour the egg mixture into the flour mixture and lightly stir together. Then fold in the cheese and pepperoni.

4 Spoon the mixture into the muffin pan. Bake for 20-25 minutes, until golden.

Carrot crunch muffins

These sweet muffins topped with crunchy oats are super tasty! They are perfect to take along to a picnic or a party.

Ingredients

1 cup all-purpose flour

2 tsp baking powder

½ tsp baking soda

⅓ cup light brown sugar

1¾oz (50g) hazelnuts, chopped

1 tbsp poppy seeds

3½oz (100g) carrot, grated

2oz (60g) golden raisins

½ tsp ground cinnamon

1 cup rolled oats

grated zest and juice of 1 large orange

¾ cup buttermilk

1 large egg, beaten

5 tbsp unsalted butter, melted

pinch of salt

Special equipment

2 x 6-hole or 1 x 12-hole muffin pans

12 paper liners

Top tip

For extra zing, use lemons instead of oranges. Or make a hole in the mixture with your finger (at Step 5) and add a chunk of white chocolate for a gooey center in the middle of each muffin.

1

Preheat the oven to 400°F (200°C).

2

In a large bowl, mix together the flour, baking powder, baking soda, and sugar. Then stir in the nuts, poppy seeds, carrot, golden raisins, cinnamon, oats, and orange zest.

3

In another bowl, mix the buttermilk, egg, butter, salt, and orange juice. Mix together well, then pour the wet ingredients into the dry.

4

Mix the wet and dry ingredients together. Don't mix it too much or the muffins won't end up light and fluffy.

5

Line the muffin pans with the liners. Spoon the mixture into the liners, filling them about two-thirds of the way full. Bake for 20–25 minutes. Move to a wire rack to cool.

Drizzle muffins

These bright and tasty lemon muffins are a real treat. They are perfect for a party or when you have friends over.

How long?   10 mins prep,
                 25 mins baking

How many?   8

Ingredients

2 lemons
2 cups self-rising flour
½ tsp baking soda
½ tsp salt
½ cup granulated sugar
2 tbsp poppy seeds
½ cup milk
1 large egg, beaten
⅓ cup sunflower oil

For the icing

⅔ cup confectioners' sugar
2 tsp lemon zest
2 tsp lemon juice

To decorate

2 tsp lemon zest
16 candied lemon slices

Special equipment

12-hole muffin pan
8 paper muffin liners
zester (optional)

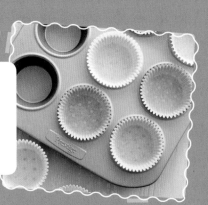

1 Preheat the oven to 375°F (190°C). Line the muffin pan with the paper liners.

2 Juice and grate one lemon and retain the juice. Add the zest to a bowl with the flour, baking soda, salt, sugar, and poppy seeds.

3 Beat the milk, egg, oil, and lemon juice in a bowl, then pour the wet ingredients into the dry and stir until just combined.

4 Spoon the mixture into the liners. Bake for 20–25 minutes, until well risen. Leave to cool on a wire rack.

5 In a small bowl, mix together the confectioners' sugar, lemon zest, and juice. Once the muffins have cooled, drizzle the icing over them.

Decorate with LEMON ZEST and CANDIED LEMON SLICES.

FRESH AND LEMONY!

Creamy cupcakes

Topped with a swirl of buttercream frosting, these delicious vanilla cupcakes are perfect for a party.

Level rating 🧁🧁

How long? 20 mins prep, 25 mins baking

How many? 24

Ingredients

1½ cups all-purpose flour, sifted
2 tsp baking powder
¾ cup granulated sugar
½ tsp salt
7 tbsp unsalted butter, softened
3 large eggs
⅔ cup milk
1 tsp vanilla extract

For the frosting

1⅔ cups confectioners' sugar
1 tsp vanilla extract
7 tbsp unsalted butter, softened
sugar sprinkles, to decorate

Special equipment

2 x 12-hole cupcake pans
24 paper cupcake liners
piping bag and star nozzle

1 Preheat the oven to 350°F (180°C).

2 Put the flour, baking powder, sugar, salt, and butter in a bowl. Rub together with your fingers until it looks like bread crumbs.

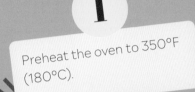

3 In another bowl, beat the eggs, milk, and vanilla extract together until well blended. Slowly pour the egg mixture into the dry ingredients, mixing all the time.

4 Beat slowly until smooth, being careful not to overmix. Pour all the cake batter into a liquid measuring cup to make it easier to handle.

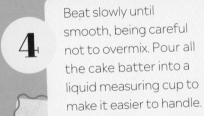

5 Put the paper liners into the cupcake pans. Carefully pour the cupcake mixture into the liners, filling each one to half full. Bake for 20–25 minutes.

6 Test the cupcakes with a skewer. Leave for a few minutes, then transfer the cupcakes to a wire rack to cool completely.

7 For the frosting, put the confectioners' sugar, vanilla extract, and butter in a bowl. Beat with an electric mixer for five minutes, until light and fluffy. Place in a piping bag fitted with a star nozzle.

8 Pipe by squeezing out the frosting with one hand, while holding the cupcake with the other.

9 Starting from the edge, pipe a spiral of frosting that comes to a peak in the center.

10 Decorate the cupcakes with sprinkles. The cupcakes will keep in an airtight container for up to three days.

Pretty cupcakes

Top these simple cupcakes with pretty decorations and have fun with your color combinations. Stacked in a tower, they are the perfect party treat.

Level rating

How long? 1 hr 15 mins prep,
2 days drying,
15 mins baking

How many? 12

Ingredients

7 tbsp unsalted butter, softened
½ cup granulated sugar
½ cup self-rising flour
2 large eggs, beaten
½ tsp vanilla extract

For the decoration and buttercream frosting

cornstarch, for dusting
7oz (200g) pink fondant
7oz (200g) white fondant
20 tbsp unsalted butter, softened
4½ cups confectioners' sugar, sifted
peach coloring paste or gel

Special equipment

fondant roller
butterfly plunger cutters, small and large
large flower plunger cutter
2 x 6-hole or 1 x 12-hole cupcake pans
12 paper cupcake liners
piping bag with large open star nozzle
12 lace cupcake wrappers

1 Dust a surface with cornstarch. Roll out the pink fondant and white fondant. Use the plunger cutters to make butterfly and flower shapes.

2 Set aside to dry for two days. Place the butterflies in the middle of an open book. This will position the wings to be open as they dry.

3 Preheat the oven to 350°F (180°C). Line the cupcake pans with the paper liners. Put the butter, sugar, flour, eggs, and vanilla extract in a bowl and beat until creamy.

4 Divide the mixture between the paper liners. Bake for 15 minutes, until golden and just firm. Cool in the pan for five minutes.

5 Move to a wire rack to cool completely.

6 For the buttercream frosting, use an electric mixer to mix the butter with the confectioners' sugar in a large bowl. Beat until smooth and fluffy.

7 Using a palette knife, smooth half the frosting onto six cupcakes. Top with fondant shapes.

8 For the six peach cupcakes, mix the food coloring paste into the remaining buttercream frosting.

9 Put the peach frosting in the piping bag, fitted with the large open star nozzle.

10 Pipe layers of frosting in a spiral movement, making each layer slightly smaller as you go. Top with the fondant shapes. Place all the cupcakes in the lace wrappers before serving.

Cupcake owl

This creation is perfect for a party or family get-together. And you can make eight mini owls to sit alongside the big owl creation.

HOO, HOO

Level rating

How long? 1 hr 15 mins prep,
15 mins baking,
20 mins drying

How many? 24

Ingredients

11 tbsp unsalted butter, softened
⅔ cup granulated sugar
½ tsp vanilla extract
3 large eggs
1¼ cups self-rising flour

For the frosting

14 tbsp unsalted butter, softened
3 cups confectioners' sugar, sifted
yellow food coloring or gel
green food coloring or gel

To top the cupcakes

1 chocolate-covered sponge cake cookie,
   cut in quarters
7oz (200g) white chocolate buttons;
   reserve one to melt
2½oz (75g) chocolate-dipped pretzels,
   snapped into thirds
1oz (25g) milk chocolate, grated
4 chocolate-covered sponge cake cookies,
   cut in half
2 large milk chocolate buttons
1 large milk chocolate button, cut in half
3½oz (100g) milk chocolate chips

Special equipment

2 x 12-hole cupcake pans
24 paper cupcake liners

1 Preheat the oven to 350°F (180°C). Put the paper liners in the cupcake pans.

2 Cream together the butter and granulated sugar in a bowl using an electric mixer until light and fluffy. Then beat in the vanilla extract.

3 Add the eggs, one at a time, beating well after each addition. Add a little flour after each addition if the mixture starts to curdle.

4 Sift in the flour. Then use a metal spoon to fold it in.

5 Spoon the mixture into the liners and bake for 15 minutes.

6 Cool the cupcakes on a wire rack.

7 Use a sharp knife to carefully level the top of each cupcake.

8 For the frosting, beat the butter with half the confectioners' sugar using an electric mixer. Then beat in the rest of the confectioners' sugar until fluffy. Divide into two portions. Use the food coloring to make one portion yellow and the other green.

9 Using a palette knife, cover the surface of 12 cupcakes with the yellow frosting. Cover the remaining 12 cupcakes with green frosting.

10 To make the beak of the owl, take one-quarter of the cookie and place it, chocolate-side down, on top of one of the green cupcakes. Place three white chocolate buttons beneath the cookie so that the buttons overlap each other.

11 For the claws, cut out V-shapes from two cookie quarters. Put a claw on two of the yellow cupcakes. Put pretzels beneath them. Cover two other yellow cupcakes with pretzels.

13 For the wings, take four green cupcakes and press two halves of the cookies on one side of each cupcake. Sprinkle grated chocolate on the remaining portion of each cupcake.

12 To make the body, cover three green cupcakes with white buttons. Take two more green cupcakes, cover half of their surface with the white buttons. Sprinkle grated chocolate on the remaining half of each.

14 For the eyes, place a large button in the middle of two yellow cupcakes. Dot melted white chocolate on each eye. For the ears, put half a large button on each cupcake. Put chocolate chips around the edges.

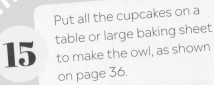

15 Put all the cupcakes on a table or large baking sheet to make the owl, as shown on page 36.

TRY THIS

• Make eight baby owl cupcakes using the leftover cupcakes. Cut eight cookies in half and use them for the wings. Use another two cookies to make the beaks by cutting small triangles from the cookies.

• Use 16 white chocolate buttons for the eyes. For the pupils, use frosting to stick chocolate chips to the eyes.

• Cut milk chocolate buttons in half for the ears and grate milk chocolate onto the torso. If needed, use extra frosting to hold the wings, beak, and ears in place.

Fudge cake balls

These bite-size treats are deliciously chocolatey and simple to make.

Ingredients

7 tbsp unsalted butter, softened,
  or soft margarine, plus extra for greasing
½ cup granulated sugar
2 large eggs
⅔ cup self-rising flour
3 tbsp cocoa powder
1 tsp baking powder
1 tbsp milk, plus extra if needed
5½oz (150g) store-bought chocolate
  fudge icing
9oz (250g) dark chocolate cake covering
1¾oz (50g) white chocolate, broken
  into pieces

Special equipment

7in (18cm) round cake pan
food processor with blade attachment

1 Preheat the oven to 350°F (180°C). Grease the pan and line the bottom and sides with parchment paper.

2 Using an electric mixer, cream the butter and sugar until fluffy. Beat in the eggs one at a time, mixing well between additions, until smooth and creamy.

3 Sift together the flour, cocoa, and baking powder, and fold into the cake batter.

4 Mix in enough milk to thin the batter so that it will drop off a spoon.

5 Spoon into the pan and bake for 25 minutes, until the surface is springy to the touch. Cool in the pan on a wire rack.

6 Pulse the cake in the processor until it looks like bread crumbs. Put 2½ cups in a bowl. Add the fudge icing and blend together to a smooth, uniform mix.

7 Using dry hands, roll the cake mix into 20–25 balls, each the size of a walnut. Put the balls on a plate and freeze for 30 minutes, until firm.

8 Line two baking sheets with parchment paper. Melt the cake covering according to the directions on the package. Put a few balls into the chocolate.

9 Using two forks, turn each ball in the chocolate until covered. Remove, allowing excess to drip off. Cover all the balls.

10 Put the coated cake balls on the baking sheets to dry.

11 Melt the white chocolate in a heatproof bowl over a pan of simmering water.

12 Drizzle the white chocolate over the balls. Leave to dry completely before moving the balls to a serving platter.

KEEP in an AIRTIGHT CONTAINER for up to THREE DAYS.

Victoria sponge cake

Popular in Britain, this tasty cake is made up of jam and buttercream frosting sandwiched between two layers of superlight and fluffy sponge cake.

Level rating

How long?   30 mins prep,
25 mins baking

How many?   6–8

Ingredients

12 tbsp unsalted butter, softened, plus extra for greasing

⅔ cup granulated sugar

3 large eggs

1 tsp vanilla extract

1 cup self-rising flour

1 tsp baking powder

For the filling

4 tbsp unsalted butter, softened

¾ cup confectioners' sugar, plus extra to serve

1 tsp vanilla extract

½ cup good-quality seedless raspberry jam

Special equipment

2 x 8in (20cm) round cake pans

1 Preheat the oven to 350°F (180°C). Grease the pans and line with parchment paper.

2 Beat the butter and sugar in a bowl for two minutes with an electric mixer, or until pale, light, and fluffy.

3 Add the eggs one at a time, mixing well between additions.

4 Add the vanilla and beat briefly until well blended. Beat the mixture for another two minutes until bubbles appear on top.

5 Sift the flour and baking powder into the bowl. With a metal spoon, gently fold in the flour until just smooth. Try to keep the mixture light.

6 Split the mixture evenly between the pans and smooth the tops with a palette knife. Bake for 20–25 minutes, or until golden brown.

7 Leave in the pans for a few minutes. Turn out, remove the parchment paper, and cool top-side up on a wire rack.

8 For the filling, beat together the butter, confectioners' sugar, and vanilla until smooth.

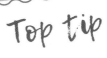

9 Spread the buttercream frosting evenly onto the flat side of a cooled sponge cake using a palette knife.

10 Gently spread the jam on top of the buttercream using a table knife.

Top tip

The filled cake will keep in an airtight container in a cool place for up to two days.

11 Top with the second sponge cake, flat sides together. Sift some confectioners' sugar on top to serve.

Chocolate cake

Everyone loves a rich chocolate cake, and in this recipe the yogurt in the mix makes it extra moist.

1 Preheat the oven to 350°F (180°C). Grease the pans and line with parchment paper.

2 Place the butter and sugar in a large bowl. Cream together with an electric mixer, until light and fluffy.

3 Crack in the eggs one at a time, beating after each addition, until well combined.

Ingredients

12 tbsp unsalted butter, softened, plus extra for greasing

1 cup light brown sugar

3 large eggs

¾ cup self-rising flour

½ cup cocoa powder

1 tsp baking powder

2 tbsp Greek yogurt or thick plain yogurt

For the chocolate buttercream

4 tbsp unsalted butter, softened

⅔ cup confectioners' sugar, sifted, plus extra to serve

¼ cup cocoa powder

a little milk, if needed

Special equipment

2 x 7in (18cm) round cake pans

4 In a separate large bowl, sift together the flour, cocoa powder, and baking powder.

5 Fold the flour mixture into the cake batter until well blended, trying to keep it light.

6 Gently fold in the yogurt. This will help to make the cake moist.

Choose a fancy PLATE or CAKE STAND to serve the cake on.

7 Split the mixture between the two pans and smooth the tops. Bake for 20–25 minutes. Leave the cakes in their pans for a few minutes. Remove the parchment and put on a wire rack top-side up.

8 For the buttercream, put the butter, confectioners' sugar, and cocoa powder in a large bowl.

9 Blend the buttercream together with an electric mixer for five minutes, or until fluffy.

10 If the cream is stiff, add milk, one teaspoon at a time, until it has a spreading consistency.

11 Spread the bottom of one sponge cake with the buttercream, then top with the other cake. Sift the confectioners' sugar over the top to serve.

Jelly roll

This tasty jam-filled cake is great to share with others. It's surprisingly easy to roll up and the swirl of jam inside looks very attractive.

Level rating

How long?   20 mins prep,
                 15 mins baking

How many?   8–10

Ingredients

3 large eggs
½ cup granulated sugar, plus extra
   for sprinkling
pinch of salt
½ cup self-rising flour
1 tsp vanilla extract

For the filling

6 tbsp raspberry jam (or any type you like)

Special equipment

13 x 9in (32.5 x 23cm) jelly roll pan

1 Preheat the oven to 400°F (200°C). Line the bottom of the pan with parchment paper.

2 Put a heatproof bowl over a pan of simmering water. Add the eggs, sugar, and salt. Beat with an electric mixer for five minutes, until thick.

3 Test the egg mixture by checking if drips from the beaters sit on the surface for a few seconds. If they do, it's ready.

4 Carefully move the bowl from the pan to a work surface. Beat for 1–2 minutes, until cool. Sift in the flour, add the vanilla extract, and gently fold in.

5 Pour the mix into the pan and gently smooth it into all the corners using a palette knife. Bake for 12–15 minutes, until firm and springy to the touch.

6 The cake is ready when it has shrunk away slightly from the sides of the pan. Sprinkle a sheet of parchment paper larger than the pan evenly with a thin layer of granulated sugar.

8 For the filling, if the jam is too thick to spread, warm it gently in a small pan. Spread the jam all over the top of the cake with a palette knife.

7 Carefully turn the cake onto the granulated sugar, so it lies upside down. Let it cool for five minutes, then peel the parchment paper from the cake.

9 Lightly press the back of a knife along one short side, ¾in (2cm) from the edge.

10 Using the pressed edge to start it off, gently but firmly roll the cake up, using the parchment paper.

11 Use the parchment to keep the cake tightly rolled and in shape. Let it cool, then unwrap the cake and place it on a serving plate, seam-side down.

Sprinkle with GRANULATED SUGAR.

Top tip
The jelly roll will keep in an airtight container for up to two days.

Chocolate chestnut roulade

The name roulade comes from the French word *rouler*, meaning "to roll." A flat cake is covered with a sweet filling before being rolled into a spiral.

Level rating

How long?   55 mins prep,
7 mins baking

How many?   8–10

Ingredients

butter, for greasing
¼ cup cocoa powder
1 tbsp all-purpose flour
pinch of salt
5 large eggs, separated into yolks
   and whites
⅔ cup granulated sugar

For the filling

4½oz (125g) chestnut puree
1oz (30g) bittersweet chocolate,
   broken into pieces
⅔ cup heavy cream
granulated sugar, to taste (optional)

For decoration

½ cup heavy cream
¼ cup granulated sugar
dark chocolate, grated with a vegetable
   peeler, to produce shavings

Special equipment

12 x 15in (30 x 37cm) jelly roll pan
piping bag and star nozzle

1 Preheat the oven to 425°F (220°C). Grease the pan and line with parchment paper. Sift the cocoa powder, flour, and salt into a large bowl.

2 In another bowl, beat the egg yolks and ⅓ cup of the sugar using an electric mixer until the mixture leaves a trail when you lift the beaters.

3 Clean the beaters. In a separate bowl, beat the egg whites until stiff. Sprinkle in the remaining sugar and beat again until glossy.

4 Sift about one-third of the cocoa mixture over the yolk mixture. Add about one-third of the egg whites.

5 Fold together lightly. Repeat with two more batches, until all the cocoa mixture and egg whites have been added.

6 Pour the batter into the pan and spread to the edges. Bake in the oven for 5-7 minutes.

7 Turn onto a damp dish towel and peel off the parchment paper. Tightly roll up the cake within the damp dish towel. Leave to cool.

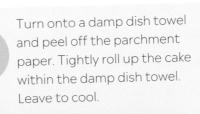

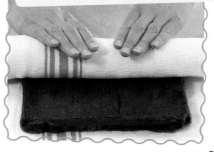

8 Put the chestnut puree in a bowl. Melt the chocolate in a heatproof bowl over a pan of simmering water. Stir the melted chocolate into the chestnut mixture.

9 Whip the cream in a separate bowl until it forms soft peaks. Fold the chestnut mixture into the whipped cream. Add sugar to taste.

10 Unroll the cake onto a piece of parchment paper. Spread on the chestnut mix using a palette knife.

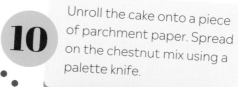

11 Using the parchment underneath, carefully roll up the filled cake as tightly as possible. Trim the edges with a serrated knife.

Decorate with the WHIPPED CREAM and CHOCOLATE SHAVINGS.

12 For the decoration, whip the cream and sugar until stiff. Fill the piping bag with the cream and decorate.

Zingy lemon polenta cake

This tasty gluten-free cake is packed with flavor and works just as well when made with wheat flour.

Ingredients

12 tbsp unsalted butter, softened, plus extra for greasing
¾ cup granulated sugar
3 large eggs, beaten
½ cup polenta or coarsely ground cornmeal
1½ cups ground almonds
finely grated zest and juice of 2 lemons
1 tsp gluten-free baking powder
pared lemon zest, to decorate
thick cream or crème fraîche, to serve (optional)

Special equipment

9in (22cm) round springform cake pan
zester (optional)

1 Preheat the oven to 325°F (160°C). Grease the pan and line the bottom with parchment paper.

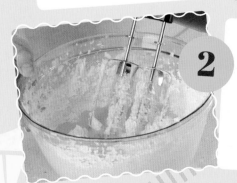

2 Cream the butter and ⅔ cup of the sugar until fluffy. Gradually pour in the eggs, a little at a time, beating well after each addition.

3 Add the polenta and almonds and gently fold into the mix, using a metal spoon.

4 Fold in the lemon zest and baking powder. The mixture will seem fairly stiff.

5 Put the mixture into the pan and smooth the surface with a palette knife.

6 Bake the cake for 50–60 minutes, until springy to the touch. Leave in the pan to cool for 10 minutes.

7 In a small saucepan, heat the lemon juice and remaining sugar over medium heat, until the sugar has dissolved completely. Take off the heat.

8 Turn the cake onto a wire rack, top-side up. Leave on the parchment for now.

9 Using a thin skewer or toothpick, poke holes in the top of the cake while still warm.

10 Pour half of the hot lemon syrup over the surface of the cake a little at a time.

11 Once the syrup has soaked into the cake, pour the rest on. Serve the cake at room temperature, on its own or with thick cream or crème fraîche.

Decorate with strips of LEMON ZEST.

Carrot cake

This sweet and crunchy cake is topped with deliciously tangy orange frosting.

Ingredients

1 cup sunflower oil, plus
  extra for greasing
3½oz (100g) walnuts
3 large eggs
1¼ cups light brown sugar
1 tsp vanilla extract
7oz (200g) carrots, finely grated
3½oz (100g) golden raisins
1½ cups self-rising flour
¾ cup whole-wheat self-rising flour
pinch of salt
1 tsp ground cinnamon
1 tsp ground ginger
¼ tsp finely grated nutmeg
finely grated zest of 1 orange

For the frosting

4 tbsp unsalted butter, softened
3½oz (100g) cream cheese, at
  room temperature
1⅔ cups confectioners' sugar
½ tsp vanilla extract
1 orange

Special equipment

9in (22cm) round springform cake pan
zester

1 Preheat the oven to 350°F (180°C). Grease the pan and line with parchment paper. Bake the walnuts on a baking sheet for five minutes. Rub the nuts with a clean dish towel to take off any excess skin.

2 Pour the oil and eggs into a large bowl, add in the sugar and the vanilla.

3 Using an electric mixer, beat the oil mixture until it is lighter and has noticeably thickened.

4 Squeeze the grated carrot thoroughly in a clean dish towel to remove excess liquid.

5 Gently fold the carrot into the cake batter, ensuring it is evenly mixed throughout.

6 Roughly chop the cooled walnuts and add to the mixture, along with the golden raisins, and gently fold them in.

7 Sift the two types of flour over the top, then add any bran left in the sieve. Add the salt, spices, and orange zest and fold all the ingredients together to combine.

8 Pour the cake mix into the pan and smooth with a palette knife. Bake for 45 minutes. Remove from the pan and take the parchment paper off. Cool on a wire rack.

9 Combine the butter, cream cheese, confectioners' sugar, and vanilla in a bowl. Grate most of the zest of the orange into the bowl, reserving some for decoration.

10 Mix all the ingredients with an electric mixer until smooth, pale, and fluffy.

11 Using a palette knife, spread the frosting over the cake. Make swirls for texture.

Use the ZESTER tool to make CURLS.

SUPER MOIST

Zesty citrus cake

Bake and decorate this beauty in less than an hour. The tangy orange taste adds a twist to a plain sponge cake.

Level rating

How long?

15 mins prep,
30 mins baking

How many?

8

Ingredients

12 tbsp unsalted butter, softened, plus extra for greasing

⅔ cup granulated sugar

3 large eggs, beaten

finely grated zest of 1 orange

1 tsp baking powder

1¼ cups self-rising flour

For the frosting

5 tbsp unsalted butter, softened

2 cups confectioners' sugar, sifted

zest of 1 orange, plus extra to decorate

2 tbsp orange juice

Special equipment

2 x 8in (20cm) cake pans

zester

1

Preheat the oven to 350°F (180°C). Grease the pans and line the bottoms with parchment paper.

Make sure to MIX IT WELL!

2

Put the butter, sugar, eggs, zest, baking powder, and flour in a large bowl. Beat together with an electric mixer until thick and well mixed.

3

Split the mix evenly between the pans and smooth the tops. Bake for 25–30 minutes.

4

Leave to cool in the pans for five minutes, then turn onto a wire rack and let the cakes cool completely.

5

To make the frosting, beat the butter, confectioners' sugar, zest, and juice in a bowl until smooth and creamy.

6

Spread half the frosting on the flat side of one of the cakes. Lay the other cake on top, flat-side down, and spread the remaining frosting over it.

Use ORANGE PEEL to DECORATE.

Slice and enjoy!

Apple cake

This sweet cake is topped with *streusel*, the German word for a crumbly topping. It makes this simple cake even tastier!

Level rating

How long?   30 mins prep,
                30 mins chilling,
                50 mins baking

How many?   8

Ingredients

12 tbsp unsalted butter, softened,
    plus extra for greasing
1 cup light brown sugar
finely grated zest of 1 lemon
3 large eggs, lightly beaten
1¼ cups self-rising flour
3 tbsp milk
2 apples, peeled, cored, and cut
    into even, slim wedges

For the streusel topping

¾ cup all-purpose flour
⅓ cup light brown sugar
2 tsp ground cinnamon
6 tbsp cold unsalted butter, diced

Special equipment

8in (20cm) loose-bottomed cake pan

1   To make the topping, put the flour, sugar, and cinnamon in a mixing bowl.

2   Rub in the butter with your fingers to form a dough. Wrap in plastic wrap and chill for 30 minutes.

3   Preheat the oven to 375°F (190°C). Grease the pan and line the bottom with parchment paper.

4   Beat the butter and sugar in a mixing bowl until pale and creamy. Add the lemon zest and beat slowly until well mixed.

5   Beat in the eggs, a little at a time, mixing well after each addition, to prevent curdling.

6   Sift the flour into the batter and gently fold in with a metal spoon. Add the milk to the batter and gently mix it in.

7 Spread half the mixture in the pan and smooth with a palette knife. Put half the apple wedges over the mixture, overlapping them slightly.

8 Spread the rest of the mixture over the apples. Then put the remaining apples on the mixture, overlapping them slightly.

9 Coarsely grate the streusel dough and sprinkle it evenly over the top of the cake.

SERVE WARM

10 Bake for 45–50 minutes. Test it with a skewer to check that it is cooked through.

11 Leave the cake to cool slightly in the pan for 10 minutes. Keeping the streusel on top, carefully remove the cake from the pan.

TO SERVE, transfer to a LARGE PLATE.

Rhubarb and ginger upside-down cake

Baked with the rhubarb at the bottom, this delicious dessert is turned upside down to serve.

Level rating

How long?   40 mins prep, 45 mins baking

How many?   6–8

Ingredients

11 tbsp unsalted butter, softened, plus extra for greasing

1lb 2oz (500g) young, pink rhubarb

¾ cup dark brown sugar

¼ cup finely chopped, preserved stem ginger or candied ginger

3 large eggs

1 cup self-rising flour

2 tsp ground ginger

1 tsp baking powder

heavy cream, whipped, or crème fraîche, to serve (optional)

Special equipment

9in (22cm) round springform cake pan

1   Preheat the oven to 350°F (180°C). Grease the pan and line the bottom and sides with parchment paper.

2   Remove any dry ends of the rhubarb stalks. Cut the rhubarb into ¾in (2cm) lengths with a sharp knife.

3   Scatter a little of the sugar and a small amount of chopped ginger evenly over the bottom of the cake pan.

4   Lay the rhubarb in the pan, tightly packed, making sure the bottom is well covered.

5   Put the butter and remaining sugar into a large bowl. Cream the butter and sugar until light and fluffy.

6   Beat in the eggs one at a time, beating as much air as possible into the mixture.

58

7 Gently fold the remaining chopped ginger into the mixture until well mixed.

8 Sift together the flour, ground ginger, and baking powder into a separate bowl.

9 Gently fold the dry ingredients into the cake mixture.

Top tip

The cake is also good cold and will keep in a cool place in an airtight container for up to two days.

10 Spoon the cake mix over the rhubarb. Bake for 45 minutes, until springy to the touch.

11 Leave the cake to cool in the pan for 20–30 minutes, before carefully turning it onto a plate. Take the parchment off and serve warm, with heavy cream.

SUPER MOIST

Lemon drizzle loaf cake

This lovely loaf cake is both sweet and sour at the same time. It's easy to make and best eaten once the lemon juice mixture has soaked into the cake.

Level rating

How long? 25 mins prep, 50 mins baking

How many? 8

Sweet treat!

Ingredients

14 tbsp butter, softened, plus extra
   for greasing
finely grated zest and juice of 2 lemons
¾ cup granulated sugar
3 large eggs, beaten
1⅓ cups self-rising flour
1 tsp baking powder
2 tbsp milk
⅓ cup granulated sugar
1 cup confectioners' sugar

Special equipment

1lb (450g) loaf pan

1

Preheat the oven to 350°F (180°C). Grease the loaf pan and line the bottom with parchment paper.

2

Put the lemon zest, butter, and granulated sugar in a mixing bowl and beat together with an electric mixer until the mixture is light and fluffy.

3

Beat in the eggs a little at a time. Sift the flour and baking powder into the bowl. Add the milk and mix together well. Pour the mixture into the loaf pan.

4

Bake for 45–50 minutes, or until a skewer comes out clean. Next, prick the top of the cake all over with a skewer. The holes will be filled in the next step.

5

Mix four teaspoons of the lemon juice with the granulated sugar. Drizzle the sugary juice over the cake so it sinks into all the holes. Allow the cake to cool before taking it out of the pan.

6

Combine the confectioners' sugar with the rest of the lemon juice and mix until smooth. Drizzle the icing over the top, allowing it to run over the sides.

Banana bread

A mash of ripe bananas is delicious baked in this sweet quick loaf. Spices and nuts add an amazing flavor and crunch.

Level rating 🧁🧁

How long? 25 mins prep, 40 mins baking

How many? 2 loaves

Ingredients

unsalted butter, for greasing

2¼ cups bread flour, plus extra for dusting

2 tsp baking powder

2 tsp ground cinnamon

1 tsp salt

4½oz (125g) walnut pieces, coarsely chopped

3 large eggs

3 ripe bananas, chopped

finely grated zest and juice of 1 lemon

½ cup vegetable oil

¾ cup granulated sugar

½ cup brown sugar

2 tsp vanilla extract

cream cheese or butter, to serve (optional)

Special equipment

2 x 1lb (450g) loaf pan

1 Preheat the oven to 350°F (180°C). Grease and flour both loaf pans thoroughly.

2 Sift the flour, baking powder, cinnamon, and salt into a large bowl. Mix in the walnuts. Make a well in the center.

3 Beat the eggs in a separate bowl with a fork or whisk.

4 Mash the bananas with a fork in another bowl until they form a smooth paste.

5 Stir the bananas into the egg mixture until well blended. Add the lemon zest and mix together.

6 Add the lemon juice, oil, both types of sugar, and vanilla. Stir until combined.

7 Pour three-quarters of the banana mixture into the well in the flour and stir well. Gradually blend in the remaining banana mixture. Stir until just smooth.

8 Spoon the mixture into the pans, dividing it equally. The pans should be about half full.

9 Bake for 35–40 minutes, until the loaves start to shrink away from the sides of the pans. Test with a skewer. It should come out clean.

10 Let the loaves cool slightly in the pans, then transfer to a wire rack to cool completely.

Top tip

This bread will keep in an airtight container for up to four days.

Serve with BUTTER or CREAM CHEESE.

Baked berry cheesecake

This delicious cheesecake is so simple to make. Served with a sweet strawberry sauce, it is definitely fit for a party.

Level rating

How long? 45 mins prep,
1 hr 10 mins baking,
4 hrs chilling

How many? 8

Ingredients

5 tbsp unsalted butter, melted, plus extra
    for greasing
5½oz (150g) graham crackers, crushed into
    fine crumbs

For the filling

1½lb (675g) cream cheese, at room
    temperature
⅔ cup sour cream, at room
    temperature
⅔ cup granulated sugar
1 tsp vanilla extract
pinch of fine sea salt
grated zest of ½ lemon
1 tbsp lemon juice
2 large eggs

For the sauce

14oz (400g) strawberries, thinly sliced
1 tbsp lemon juice
1 tbsp granulated sugar
¼ cup strawberry jam, sieved to
    remove seeds

Special equipment

8in (20cm) deep springform cake pan

1 Preheat the oven to 350°F (180°C). Grease the bottom and sides of the pan and line with parchment paper. Combine the melted butter with the graham cracker crumbs in a large bowl.

2 Pour the mixture into the pan. Using the back of a spoon, gently press it into the bottom of the pan to form an even layer. Bake for 10 minutes, then set aside to cool.

3 For the filling, whisk the cream cheese, sour cream, sugar, vanilla extract, salt, and lemon zest and juice in a bowl until combined. Add the eggs, one at a time, and whisk well to combine.

4 Cover the bottom and sides of the pan with foil and put it in a large roasting pan. Pour the filling over the cracker crust. Pour enough boiling water into the roasting pan to come halfway up the sides of the pan.

5 Bake for one hour. Turn off the oven and leave the cheesecake to cool in the oven for 30 minutes. Let it cool completely on a wire rack, then chill for at least four hours.

TRY THIS

Instead of using strawberries for the sauce, you can use the same weight of raspberries, blueberries, or blackberries.

6 For the sauce, mix the strawberries, lemon juice, and sugar in a bowl, then leave for 30 minutes. Gently heat the jam in a small saucepan. Stir it into the strawberry mixture and let cool. Drizzle the sauce over the cheesecake to serve.

Top tip

The cheesecake will keep in the fridge, well wrapped in plastic wrap, for up to three days.

Marbled chocolate cheesecake

This mouthwatering cheesecake is perfect for any special occasion. The marble effect is unique, since it varies each time you make the cake.

Ingredients

5 tbsp unsalted butter, melted, plus extra
  for greasing
5½oz (150g) graham crackers, crushed
5½oz (150g) bittersweet chocolate
1lb 2oz (500g) full-fat cream cheese,
  at room temperature
⅔ cup granulated sugar
1 tsp vanilla extract
2 large eggs

Special equipment

8in (20cm) deep springform cake pan

1 Grease the bottom and sides of the pan with melted butter. Mix the crushed crackers and melted butter together in a bowl with a wooden spoon. Press the mixture over the bottom and sides of the pan. Chill for 30–60 minutes, until firm.

2 Preheat the oven to 350°F (180°C).

3 Break the chocolate into chunks, then melt it in a heatproof bowl placed over a pan of simmering water, stirring occasionally, until smooth. Leave it to cool.

4 Beat the cream cheese in a bowl with an electric mixer for 2–3 minutes, until smooth. Add the sugar and vanilla extract, and beat again until smooth. Add the eggs one by one, beating well after each addition. Pour half of the filling into the graham cracker crust.

5 Once the melted chocolate has completely cooled, mix it into the remaining filling.

6 Carefully spoon the chocolate filling in a ring over the plain filling.

7 Using a table knife, swirl the fillings together to make a marbled pattern. Bake in the oven for 50–60 minutes, until the side is set. Turn the oven off and leave the cake in there until cool. Chill for four hours before serving.

TRY THIS

For an all-chocolate cheesecake, use 10oz (300g) bittersweet or white chocolate, ½ cup sugar, and don't divide the mixture.

Top tip

This cheesecake can be made up to three days ahead, kept tightly wrapped in plastic wrap in the fridge.

Blueberry ripple cheesecake

The marbled effect on this cheesecake is so easy to achieve and always looks magical. Serve it with a *compote*, the French word for a fruity sauce.

Level rating

How long?   30 mins prep,
40 mins baking,
1 hr setting time

How many?   8

Ingredients

4 tbsp unsalted butter,
   plus extra for greasing
4½oz (125g) graham crackers
5½oz (150g) blueberries
⅔ cup granulated sugar, plus 3 tbsp extra
14oz (400g) cream cheese
9oz (250g) mascarpone
2 large eggs, plus 1 large egg yolk
½ tsp vanilla extract
2 tbsp all-purpose flour, sifted

For the compote

3½oz (100g) blueberries
1 tbsp granulated sugar
squeeze of lemon juice

Special equipment

8in (20cm) deep springform cake pan
food processor with blade attachment
nylon sieve

1 Preheat the oven to 350°F (180°C). Grease the bottom and sides of the cake pan.

2 Put the crackers in a food bag and crush with a rolling pin to make into crumbs. Melt the butter in a saucepan over low heat. It should not begin to turn brown.

3 Add the crumbs to the pan and stir until they are coated in butter. Remove from the heat. Press the crumbs down into the bottom of the cake pan, using the back of a spoon.

4 Put the blueberries and three tablespoons of sugar in the processor. Pulse until smooth. Push the mix through the nylon sieve into a small pan. Boil and then simmer for 3–5 minutes. Carefully take off the heat.

5 Place the remaining sugar, cream cheese, mascarpone, eggs, yolk, vanilla, and flour in the processor. Pulse until smooth. Pour the mix onto the graham cracker crust and smooth the top.

6 Drizzle the berry mixture over the top and make swirls by drawing a metal skewer through the mix.

7 Boil a kettle of water. Wrap the sides of the cake pan with foil. Put it in a deep roasting pan. Pour hot water into the pan, to come halfway up the cake pan.

8 Bake for 40 minutes until set, but a little wobbly. Turn off the oven, open the door, and leave the cake inside the oven for one hour. Put the cake on a wire rack and take off the sides of the pan.

9 Use two cake slicers to move the cheesecake to a serving platter and leave to cool completely.

10 Put all the ingredients for the compote in a small pan and heat it gently until the sugar dissolves. Carefully transfer to a pitcher to serve.

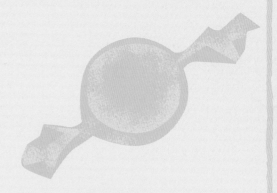

CELEBRATION CAKES

Create amazing "Wow!" confections that will impress your friends and family. Perfect for parties and festive occasions, these luxurious layered cakes are rich, sweet, and full of surprises.

Triple-layer chocolate cake

If you are a chocolate lover, you will adore this cake. The rich sponge cake is topped with mouthwatering icing and delicious chocolate curls.

Ingredients

20 tbsp unsalted butter, softened,
   plus extra for greasing
1¼ cups granulated sugar
1¾ cups self-rising flour
¼ cup cocoa powder
1 tsp baking soda
5 large eggs
1 tsp vanilla extract
¼ cup milk

For the icing and filling

6oz (175g) bittersweet chocolate
1¾ cups heavy cream
2 tbsp unsalted butter
1 tbsp granulated sugar
a few drops of vanilla extract

Special equipment

3 x 8in (20cm) cake pans

1 Preheat the oven to 350°F (180°C). Lightly grease the pans and line the bottoms with parchment paper.

2 Put the butter and sugar in a large bowl and beat with an electric mixer until pale. Sift the flour, cocoa powder, and baking soda into the bowl. Add the eggs, vanilla extract, and milk, then beat for one minute, until the mixture is fluffy.

3 Divide the mixture evenly between the three pans and level the surface. Bake for 30–35 minutes, until the sponge cakes spring back when lightly pressed. Leave the cakes to cool in the pans for five minutes, then move to a wire rack to cool completely.

4 To make the chocolate curls, break off 1¾oz (50g) of the chocolate. Carefully draw a vegetable peeler across the surface of the chocolate at an angle so that curls of chocolate form. Set aside in a cool place.

5 Put the remaining chocolate and ⅔ cup of the cream in a heatproof bowl set over a pan of gently simmering water. Stir until the chocolate melts. Remove from the heat, stir in the butter, and leave to cool.

6 In a separate bowl, beat the remaining cream, sugar, and vanilla extract with an electric mixer, until soft peaks form. Spread the cream on two of the cakes, stack them on top of each other, then top with the third cake.

7 Spoon the cooled chocolate icing over the top, allowing a little to drip down the sides of the cake. Scatter the chocolate curls over the top and serve.

Naked cake

A naked cake is easy to spot, with its bare layers and simple decoration. This one has tasty freeze-dried raspberries and a lemon flavor that make it the ideal cake for any party.

Level rating

How long? 1 hr prep,
30 mins baking

How many? 12–14

Ingredients

24 tbsp unsalted butter, cubed and
softened, plus extra for greasing

1½ cups granulated sugar

finely grated zest of 2 lemons

6 large eggs

2½ cups self-rising flour

2 tbsp milk

½oz (15g) freeze-dried raspberries, plus
extra to decorate

For the frosting

10 tbsp unsalted butter, softened

finely grated zest of 1 lemon

2 cups confectioners' sugar

7oz (200g) mascarpone

2 tbsp lemon juice

fresh edible flowers, to decorate (optional)

Special equipment

3 x 8in (20cm) round cake pans

1 Preheat the oven to 350°F (180°C). Lightly grease the cake pans and line the bottoms with parchment paper.

2 Cream together the butter, sugar, and lemon zest, using an electric mixer, until light and fluffy.

3 Add the eggs, one at a time, beating well after each addition. If the mixture starts to split, add a little flour.

4 Gently fold in the flour, using a metal spoon.

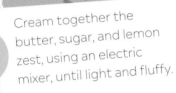

5 Stir the milk into the mixture until well combined.

6 Scatter the freeze-dried raspberries over the top and mix them in evenly.

7 Divide the mixture equally between the pans and level the tops using a spatula.

The cakes will be RISEN and SPRINGY.

8 Bake for 25–30 minutes, until the cakes are golden and springy to the touch. Swap the pans around in the oven after 15 minutes so they bake evenly.

Make sure they COOL COMPLETELY!

9 Put on wire racks to cool and take off the parchment paper.

10 For the frosting, put the butter, zest, and half the confectioners' sugar in a bowl and beat together with an electric mixer until creamy.

11 Add the mascarpone, lemon juice, and the remaining confectioners' sugar and beat until smooth and fluffy.

This gives the cake its NAKED look.

12 Once cooled, carefully level the cakes with a serrated knife. Place a slightly smaller cake pan bottom on top of each cake and use a sharp knife to cut around the edge of each cake.

13 Put a dollop of frosting onto a plate and sit one of the cakes on top. Spread with a third of the frosting.

14 Top with the next cake layer, spread on another third of the frosting, then top with the last sponge cake. Spread the remaining frosting thinly over the top.

15 Sprinkle some extra freeze-dried raspberries on top and decorate with edible flowers, if using. Serve immediately.

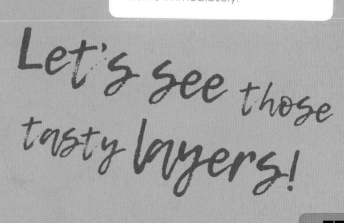

Let's see those tasty layers!

Piñata cake

Surprise your friends with this light and fluffy vanilla-flavored sponge cake filled with delicious candies. They won't be expecting goodies to be hidden inside!

Level rating

How long? 1½ hrs prep,
30 mins baking,
20 mins chilling

How many? 12–14

Ingredients

24 tbsp unsalted butter, softened,
    plus extra for greasing
1½ cups granulated sugar
2 tsp vanilla extract
6 large eggs
2½ cups self-rising flour

For the frosting, filling, and decoration

20 tbsp unsalted butter, softened
5 cups confectioners' sugar, sifted
pink, orange, yellow, and blue food coloring
    gels or pastes
colored candies, to fill
cake bunting, to decorate (optional)

Special equipment

3 x 8in (20cm) round cake pans
3 x piping bags and star nozzles
3in (7.5cm) round cookie cutter

1

Preheat the oven to 350°F (180°C). Lightly grease the pans and line the bottoms with parchment paper.

2

Cream together the butter and granulated sugar with an electric mixer until light and fluffy. Then beat in the vanilla.

3

Add the eggs, one at a time, beating well after each addition.

4

Gently fold in the flour using a metal spoon.

5

Divide the mixture evenly in the three pans, weighing them to ensure they are equal. Bake for 25–30 minutes, until golden.

6 Take the cakes out of the pans, peel off the parchment paper, and cool on wire racks.

7 To make the frosting, beat the butter with half the confectioners' sugar, then beat in the rest until light and fluffy. Add 1–2 teaspoons hot water to make the frosting spreadable.

Be CAREFUL when CUTTING the CAKE.

9 Cut out the centers of two of the cakes using the cookie cutter. You can make a small cake with the centers, or use them in a trifle.

8 When the cakes are cool, carefully level the tops using a serrated knife.

SPREAD the FROSTING to the EDGES.

10 Mix a quarter of the frosting with the pink coloring. Place the first ring onto a serving platter and sandwich together with the next ring, using a layer of pink frosting. Put more pink frosting on the second ring.

11 Fill the center of the cake with the candies. Place the remaining uncut cake on top to make the top level.

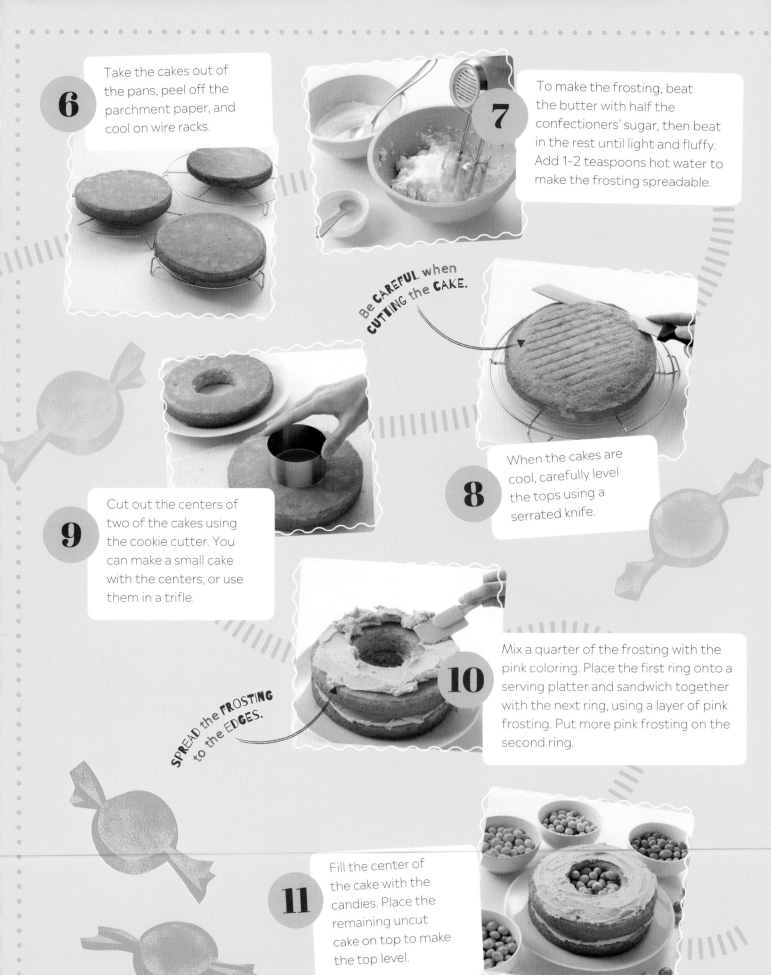

12 Spread the sides and top of the cake with a thin layer of plain frosting, taking care not to get crumbs in the bowl of frosting. Chill for 20 minutes. This helps the frosting stick to the cake.

13 Spread a little more plain frosting around the edge and over the top of the cake.

Choose DIFFERENT COLORS if you LIKE.

14 Divide the remaining frosting between three bowls and color each bowl with a different food coloring. Put the frosting into three piping bags that are each fitted with a star nozzle.

Use CANDIES to TOP the BUNTING POLES.

15 Pipe alternating colors of frosting in a ring around the edge on top of the cake. Stick the bunting on top to decorate, if using.

supersweet surprise!

Mini red velvets

These lovely little red cakes are made up of a light sponge cake and yummy cream cheese frosting. Topped with fresh raspberries, they are perfect to show off at any special occasion.

1 Preheat the oven to 325°F (160°C). Lightly grease and flour the cake pans.

2 Put the flour, cocoa powder, baking soda, and baking powder in a bowl and mix together.

3 In a separate bowl, cream together the butter and sugar with an electric mixer for 2–3 minutes, until light and fluffy.

4 Beat in the vanilla and red food coloring until the color is evenly blended. Beat in the egg with a spoonful of the flour mixture.

Ingredients

7 tbsp buttery spread or unsalted butter, softened, plus extra for greasing

¾ cup all-purpose flour, plus extra for dusting

1 tbsp cocoa powder, sifted

½ tsp baking soda

1 tsp baking powder

½ cup granulated sugar

1 tsp vanilla extract

3–4 tsp red gel food coloring

1 large egg, beaten

½ cup buttermilk

½ tsp distilled white vinegar

For the cream cheese frosting

7 tbsp unsalted butter, softened

3½oz (100g) cream cheese

3½ cups confectioners' sugar, sifted

1 tsp lemon juice

fresh raspberries or red sprinkles, to decorate

Special equipment

16 mini cake pans, about 2½ x 1in (6.5 x 2.5cm), or 3 x 6-hole muffin pans

piping bag and star nozzle

5 Stir in half the buttermilk, then a spoon of the flour mixture. Alternate adding the buttermilk and flour mixture until all the ingredients are mixed in. Stir in the vinegar.

6 Spoon the mixture into the pans until half full (or less if using a muffin pan; only fill 16 holes). Bake for 8–10 minutes.

7 Let the cakes cool in the pans for a few minutes, then put on a wire rack. Let them cool completely before frosting.

8 To make the frosting, beat together the butter and cream cheese, then beat in the confectioners' sugar a little at a time.

9 Once all the confectioners' sugar has been added, beat in the lemon juice until the mixture is paler in color.

10 Use some of the frosting to sandwich two of the cakes together. Repeat with the other cakes. Pipe the remaining frosting on top of each cake. Decorate with raspberries or sprinkles.

Black Forest cake

This traditional German cake is a mouthwatering blend of rich dark chocolate and sweet cherries. It definitely deserves its place on a celebration table.

Level rating 🧁🧁🧁

How long? 55 mins prep,
40 mins baking

How many? 8–10

Ingredients

6 tbsp unsalted butter, melted, plus
    extra for greasing
6 large eggs
⅔ cup granulated sugar
¾ cup all-purpose flour
½ cup cocoa powder
1 tsp vanilla extract

For the filling and decoration

2 x 15oz (425g) cans pitted black cherries,
    drained, 10 tbsp juice reserved, and
    cherries from 1 can roughly chopped
2½ cups heavy cream
5½oz (150g) dark chocolate, grated

Special equipment

9in (22cm) round springform cake pan
piping bag and star nozzle

1 Preheat the oven to 350°F (180°C). Grease the pan and line the bottom and sides with parchment paper.

2 Put the eggs and sugar into a large heatproof bowl that will fit over a saucepan.

3 Place the bowl over a pan of simmering water. Don't let the bowl touch the water.

4 Mix with an electric mixer until the mixture is pale and thick and will hold a trail from the beaters.

5 Remove from the heat and beat for another five minutes, or until cooled slightly.

6 Sift in the flour and cocoa. Gently fold into the egg mixture using a spatula. Fold in the vanilla and butter.

7 Pour the cake mixture into the pan and level the surface.

8 Bake for 40 minutes, or until risen and just shrinking away from the sides.

9 Put on a wire rack, peel off the parchment paper, and cover with a clean cloth. Let it cool.

10 Carefully cut the cake into three layers. Use a serrated knife and long sweeping strokes.

11 Drizzle a third of the reserved cherry juice over each layer of the cake.

12 Whip the cream in a separate bowl until it just holds soft peaks; it should not be too stiff.

13 Place a layer of cake on a plate. Spread with the cream and half the chopped cherries.

14 Repeat with the second layer of cake. Top with the final cake layer, right-side up. Gently press down.

15 Cover the side with a layer of cream. Put the leftover cream in the piping bag.

16 Press grated chocolate onto the creamy sides using a palette knife.

17 Pipe a ring of cream swirls around the cake and place the whole cherries inside the ring.

Top tip

The cake can be covered and kept in the fridge for up to three days.

Festive fruit cake

This recipe makes a wonderfully moist, rich fruit cake, ideal for Christmas, weddings, baptisms, and birthdays.

Top tip

This cake will keep, un-iced, for up to eight weeks.

Ingredients

7oz (200g) golden raisins

14oz (400g) raisins

12oz (350g) prunes, chopped

12oz (350g) candied cherries

2 small sweet apples, peeled, cored, and diced

2½ cups apple juice

4 tsp pumpkin pie spice

14 tbsp unsalted butter, softened

1 cup dark brown sugar

3 large eggs, beaten

1⅓ cups ground almonds

1¾ cups all-purpose flour, plus extra for dusting

2 tsp baking powder

For the frosting

14oz (400g) store-bought marzipan

2–3 tbsp apricot jam

3 large egg whites

4 cups confectioners' sugar

Special equipment

8–10in (20–25cm) deep round cake pan

1. Put the golden raisins, raisins, prunes, cherries, apples, juice, and spice in a saucepan.

2. Simmer over medium-low heat and cover for 20 minutes, until most of the liquid is absorbed.

3. Take off the heat. Leave overnight at room temperature for the fruits to absorb the liquid fully.

4. Preheat the oven to 325°F (160°C). Double-line the bottom and sides of the pan with parchment paper.

5. Using an electric mixer, cream the butter and sugar in a large bowl, until fluffy.

6. Add the eggs, a little at a time, beating very well after each addition to prevent the mixture from curdling.

7. Gently fold in the fruit mix and ground almonds, trying to keep volume in the mixture.

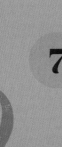

8 Sift the flour and baking powder into the bowl and gently fold into the mixture.

9 Spoon the mixture into the pan, cover with foil, and bake for two and a half hours.

10 Test that the cake is ready: a skewer inserted into the center should come out clean.

11 Let cool, then turn the cake onto a wire rack to cool completely. Peel off the parchment paper.

12 Trim the cake to level it. Transfer to a stand and hold in place with some marzipan.

13 Warm the jam and brush it thickly over the whole cake. This will help the marzipan stick.

14 On a lightly floured surface, knead the remaining marzipan until softened.

15 Roll out the softened marzipan until wide enough to cover the cake.

16 Drape the marzipan over the rolling pin and lift it over the cake.

17 With your hands or a smoother, gently ease the marzipan into place, smoothing out any bumps.

18 With a small sharp knife, carefully cut away any excess marzipan from the bottom of the cake.

19 Place the egg whites in a bowl and sift in the confectioners' sugar, stirring well to combine.

20 With an electric mixer, beat the confectioners' sugar mixture for 10 minutes, until stiff.

21 Spread the frosting over the cake with a palette knife before serving.

Painted cake

Get your paintbrush out—you're about to make an impressive edible work of art! This soft and fragrant cake is almost too beautiful to eat.

Perfect strokes

Top tip
Make sure to buy edible gold leaf and gold glitter.

Level rating

How long? 1 hr 15 mins prep,
25 mins baking,
35 mins chilling

How many? 12–14

Ingredients

20 tbsp unsalted butter, softened and
cubed, plus extra for greasing

1¼ cups granulated sugar

1 tsp rosewater extract

6 large eggs

1 cup self-rising flour

1 tsp baking powder

1 cup ground almonds

For the frosting

20 tbsp unsalted butter, softened

5 cups confectioners' sugar, sifted

1 tsp rosewater extract

pink, red, orange, and yellow food coloring
or gel

edible gold leaf, to decorate

edible gold glitter, to decorate

dried rose petals, to decorate

Special equipment

3 x 7in (18cm) round cake pans

frosting scraper

paintbrush, new and clean

1 Preheat the oven to 350°F
(180°C). Lightly grease the
pans and line the bottoms with
parchment paper.

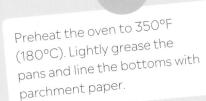

2 Using an electric mixer,
cream together the
butter and granulated
sugar until light and
fluffy. Then beat in the
rosewater extract.

3 Add the eggs one at a
time, beating well and using
an electric mixer to combine.
Add a little flour after each
addition if the mixture
starts to curdle.

4 Using a metal spoon,
fold in the flour,
baking powder, and
ground almonds.

5 Divide the mixture equally between the three pans. Bake for 20-25 minutes, until golden and springy.

6 Let the cakes cool in the pans for 10 minutes,. Peel off the parchment paper and let cool on wire racks.

7 To make the frosting, beat the butter with half the confectioners' sugar, using an electric mixer, then beat in the rest of the confectioners' sugar until light and fluffy. Mix in one teaspoon of rosewater extract and 1-2 teaspoons of hot water to make it spreadable.

8 Take a quarter of the frosting and gradually add pink food coloring until you have a soft pink frosting.

ONLY take a THIN LAYER OFF the TOP.

9 When the cakes are cool, carefully level the tops, using a serrated knife.

SPREAD to the EDGES using a PALETTE KNIFE.

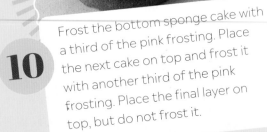

10 Frost the bottom sponge cake with a third of the pink frosting. Place the next cake on top and frost it with another third of the pink frosting. Place the final layer on top, but do not frost it.

11 Thinly cover the outside and top of the cake with some of the plain frosting, then scrape off the excess with a frosting scraper and discard. Chill in the fridge for 20 minutes to firm up.

12 Use the plain frosting to cover the cake with a final coat, smoothing the sides and top again with a frosting scraper. Chill for another 15 minutes.

14 Using a small palette knife, put dollops of frosting on the sides and top of the cake. Try to alternate the four colors.

13 Divide the remaining plain frosting between three small bowls. Use the food coloring to make one red, one orange, and one yellow.

15 Smooth the sides with a frosting scraper so the colors start to merge, then smooth the top.

Pretty *palette*

16 Use the paintbrush to add pieces of gold leaf. Spray with gold glitter and sprinkle the dried rose petals over the top of the cake.

Ice cream cone drip cake

Trick everyone with this clever party cake. The shiny ganache flowing from the upside down cone makes it appear as if the ice cream is spilling everywhere. Have a napkin ready!

TASTY, GOOEY TREAT

Level rating

How long?   1 hr 15 mins prep,
25 mins baking,
45 mins chilling

How many?   12–14

Ingredients

20 tbsp unsalted butter, softened,
   plus extra for greasing
1¼ cups granulated sugar
2 tsp vanilla extract
6 large eggs
1¾ cups self-rising flour
1 tsp baking powder

For the buttercream frosting

20 tbsp softened unsalted butter
5 cups confectioners' sugar, sifted
1 tsp raspberry or strawberry flavoring
blue food coloring or gel

For the ganache drip icing

5½oz (150g) white chocolate bark,
   broken into pieces
½ cup heavy cream
1 tsp raspberry or strawberry flavoring
pink food coloring or gel

To top the cake

ice cream cone
1–2 tbsp sprinkles

Special equipment

3 x 8in (20cm) round cake pans

1 Preheat the oven to 350°F (180°C). Lightly grease the pans and line the bottoms with parchment paper.

2 Cream together the butter and granulated sugar, using an electric mixer, until light and fluffy. Then beat in the vanilla extract.

3 Add the eggs, one at a time, beating well after each addition. Add a little flour after each addition if the mixture starts to curdle.

4 Sift in the flour and baking powder. Then use a metal spoon to fold them in.

5 Divide the mixture equally between the three pans, weighing to ensure they are equal. Bake for 20–25 minutes, until golden.

6 Let the cakes cool in the pans for 10 minutes, then remove the parchment paper and cool on a wire rack.

7 For the buttercream frosting, beat the butter with half the confectioners' sugar, using an electric mixer. Then beat in the rest of the confectioners' sugar, until light and fluffy.

8 Add the flavoring and enough blue coloring to make a bright blue frosting. Add 1–2 teaspoons of hot water to make it spreadable.

MAKE it as FLAT as you can.

9 When the cakes are cool, carefully level the tops, using a serrated knife. Keep the cake pieces.

Use your FINGERS to CRUMBLE!

10 Crumble ¾ cup of the cake tops into a bowl, then add 2–3 tablespoons of the buttercream frosting and stir gently to combine.

11 Using an ice cream scoop, shape the crumbled cake mixture into a ball, place on a small plate, and chill for 10 minutes.

12 Divide a third of the frosting between two of the cooled sponge cakes. Spread to the edges with a palette knife. Stack the cakes in three tiers with the un-frosted one on top.

13 Thinly cover the outside and top of the cake with a little more frosting, then scrape off the excess with a palette knife and discard. Chill in the fridge for 20 minutes to firm up.

14 Move the cake to a serving platter before frosting. Use most of the buttercream to cover the cake with a final coat, smoothing the sides and top using a palette knife.

15 Spread a layer of the buttercream frosting over the cake ball and chill for 10 minutes.

16 For the ganache, place the chocolate and cream in a small saucepan and cook over low heat, stirring until the chocolate has melted.

17 Take off the heat and stir in the flavoring and enough pink coloring to make a bright-pink shiny frosting. Let it cool for 3–4 minutes, to thicken.

18 Put the cake ball on top, then spoon over a little of the ganache icing to cover. Spoon the remaining icing over the top of the cake, so it starts to drip down the sides.

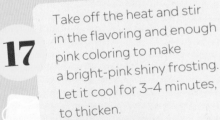

19 Scatter the sprinkles over the cake ball and at the bottom of the cake. Put an ice cream cone at an angle on top of the ball. Let it set in a cool place (not in the fridge) for 20 minutes before slicing.

PASTRIES, PIES, AND TARTS

Show off your cooking skills with creamy profiteroles and perfectly flaky pastries that melt in your mouth! Jazz up picnics and lunches with flavor-filled pies, hearty pasties, and impressive mini tartlets.

Chocolate profiteroles

The perfect choux pastry is always light and fluffy. Make these delicious buns, drizzled with chocolate sauce, as a dessert or party dish.

Level rating

How long?   30 mins prep,
                 22 mins baking

How many?   18

Ingredients

½ cup all-purpose flour

4 tbsp unsalted butter

2 eggs, beaten

For the filling and topping

1¾ cups heavy cream

7oz (200g) good-quality dark chocolate,
  broken into pieces

2 tbsp unsalted butter

2 tbsp golden syrup

Special equipment

2 piping bags with a ½in (1cm) plain nozzle
  and a ¼in (5mm) star nozzle

Serve the **BUNS** on a serving
tray or cake stand.

1

Preheat the oven to 425°F (220°C). Line two large baking sheets with parchment paper.

2

Sift the flour into a large bowl, holding the sifter up high to get air into the flour.

3

Put the butter and ⅔ cup water into a small saucepan and heat gently until melted.

4

Bring to a boil, take off the heat, and pour in the flour all at once.

5

Beat with a wooden spoon until smooth. The mixture should form a ball. Cool for 10 minutes.

6 Gradually add the eggs, beating very well after each addition.

7 Continue adding the eggs, little by little, to form a stiff, smooth, and shiny paste.

8 Spoon the mixture into a piping bag fitted with a ½in (1cm) plain nozzle.

9 Pipe 18 walnut-sized rounds onto the lined baking sheets, placing them far apart. Bake for 20 minutes, until risen and golden.

Top tip

The unfilled buns will keep in an airtight container for up to two days.

10 Take the pastry out of the oven and slit the side of each bun to allow the steam to escape.

11 Put the buns back in the oven for two minutes, to crisp, then put on a wire rack to cool completely.

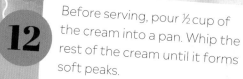

13 Add the chocolate, butter, and syrup to the cream in the pan and heat gently until melted.

12 Before serving, pour ½ cup of the cream into a pan. Whip the rest of the cream until it forms soft peaks.

14 Put the whipped cream into a piping bag fitted with a ¼in (5mm) star nozzle.

15 Put the buns on a serving platter. Fill them with the whipped cream. Drizzle the chocolate mixture over them and serve immediately.

SWEET AND CREAMY

Croissants

Although these French pastries take some time to make, the final result is well worth the effort. Start making them the day before you want to serve them.

serve with jam

Level rating

How long? 1 hr prep, 5 hrs chilling, plus overnight chilling, 1 hr rising, 20 mins baking

How many? 12

Ingredients

2½ cups bread flour, plus extra for dusting

½ tsp salt

2 tbsp granulated sugar

2½ tsp dried yeast

vegetable oil, for greasing

18 tbsp unsalted butter, chilled

1 large egg, beaten

jam, to serve

Top tip

The croissants will keep in an airtight container for up to two days. Gently reheat to serve.

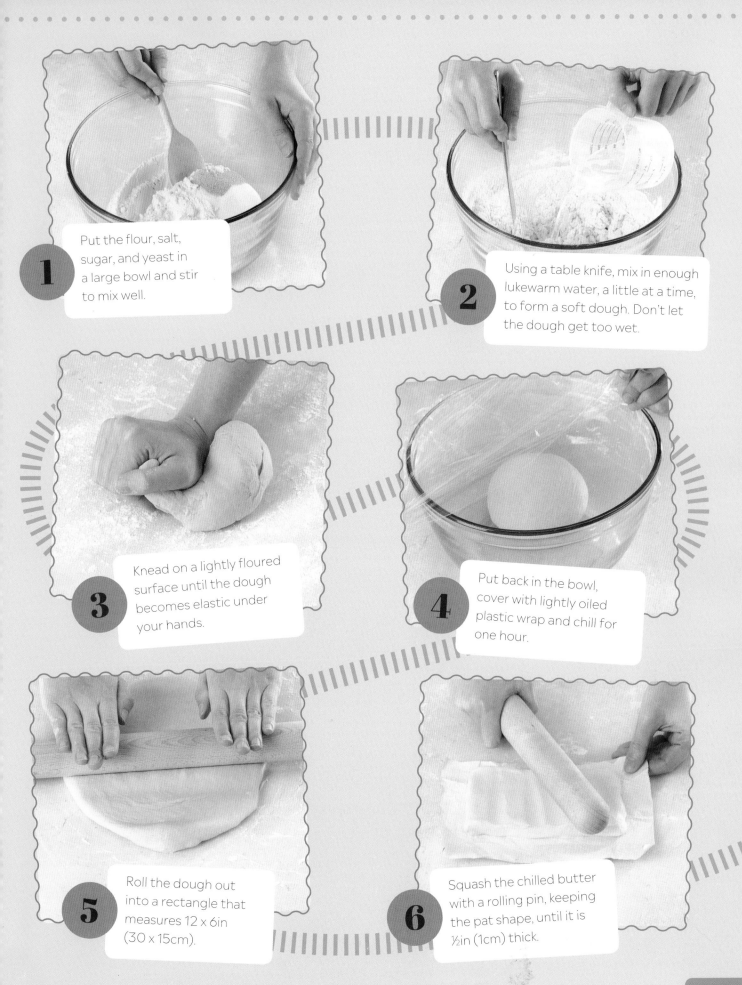

1 Put the flour, salt, sugar, and yeast in a large bowl and stir to mix well.

2 Using a table knife, mix in enough lukewarm water, a little at a time, to form a soft dough. Don't let the dough get too wet.

3 Knead on a lightly floured surface until the dough becomes elastic under your hands.

4 Put back in the bowl, cover with lightly oiled plastic wrap and chill for one hour.

5 Roll the dough out into a rectangle that measures 12 x 6in (30 x 15cm).

6 Squash the chilled butter with a rolling pin, keeping the pat shape, until it is ½in (1cm) thick.

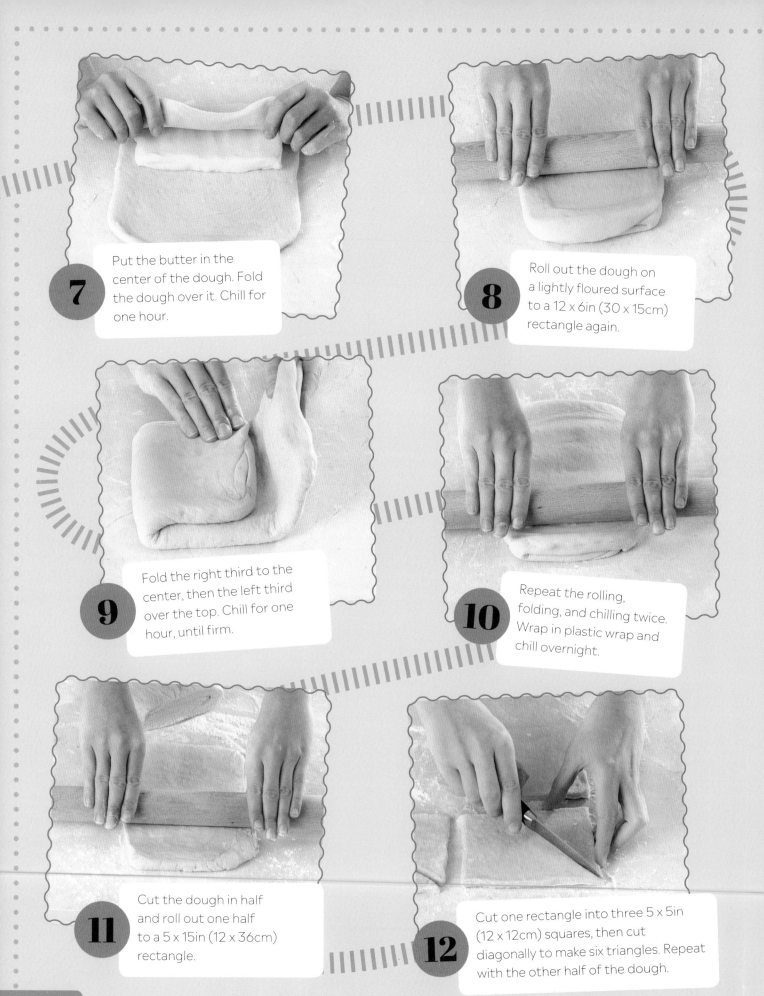

7 Put the butter in the center of the dough. Fold the dough over it. Chill for one hour.

8 Roll out the dough on a lightly floured surface to a 12 x 6in (30 x 15cm) rectangle again.

9 Fold the right third to the center, then the left third over the top. Chill for one hour, until firm.

10 Repeat the rolling, folding, and chilling twice. Wrap in plastic wrap and chill overnight.

11 Cut the dough in half and roll out one half to a 5 x 15in (12 x 36cm) rectangle.

12 Cut one rectangle into three 5 x 5in (12 x 12cm) squares, then cut diagonally to make six triangles. Repeat with the other half of the dough.

13 Holding the ends of the longest side of a triangle, roll it toward you. Curve into semicircle shapes.

14 Line two baking sheets with parchment paper and place the croissants on the sheets, leaving space between each.

15 Cover with lightly oiled plastic wrap. Leave for one hour, until doubled in size. Remove the plastic wrap.

16 Preheat the oven to 425°F (220°C). Brush the croissants with the egg, then bake for 10 minutes.

17 Lower the temperature to 375°F (190°C) and bake for another 5–10 minutes, until golden.

Rich and buttery!

Danish pastries

These tasty pastries are sweeter than the classic croissant. And the home-baked flavor is just too good to resist!

sweet treats

Level rating 🧁🧁🧁

How long? 30 mins prep, 30 mins rising, 1 hr chilling, 20 mins baking

How many? 18

Ingredients

⅔ cup lukewarm milk

2 tsp dried yeast

2 tbsp granulated sugar

2 large eggs, plus 1 egg for glazing

3¾ cups bread flour, sifted, plus extra for dusting

½ tsp salt

vegetable oil, for greasing

18 tbsp chilled butter

7oz (200g) good-quality cherry, strawberry, or apricot jam

1 Mix together the milk, yeast, and one tablespoon of the sugar. Cover with plastic wrap and leave for 20 minutes, then beat in the eggs.

2 Put the flour, salt, and remaining sugar in a bowl. Make a well and pour in the yeast mix.

3 Mix the ingredients into a soft dough. Knead for 15 minutes on a floured surface until soft.

Shape the dough INTO A BALL.

4 Put the dough in a lightly oiled bowl, cover with plastic wrap and chill for 15 minutes.

5 On a lightly floured surface, roll the dough out to a square, about 10 x 10in (25 x 25cm).

6 Cut the butter into three to four slices, each about 5 x 2½ x ½in (12 x 6 x 1cm).

7 Lay the butter slices on one half of the dough, leaving a border of ½–¾in (1–2cm).

8 Fold the other half of the dough over the top, pressing the edges with a rolling pin to seal the butter in.

9 Generously flour and roll the dough into a rectangle three times as long as it is wide and ½in (1cm) thick.

10 Fold the top third down into the middle, then the bottom third back over it.

11 Wrap in plastic wrap and chill for 15 minutes. Repeat steps 9–10 twice, chilling for 15 minutes each time. Then cut the dough in half.

12 Roll each half on a floured surface to 12 x 12in (30 x 30cm) squares, ¼–½in (5mm–1cm) thick. Cut these into nine 4 x 4in (10 x 10cm) squares, making 18 squares in total.

13 With a sharp knife, carefully make diagonal cuts from each corner to within ½in (1cm) of the center.

14 Put one teaspoon of jam in the center of each square and fold each corner into the center.

15 Spoon more jam on the center, transfer to a lined baking sheet, and cover with a dish towel.

16 Leave in a warm place for 30 minutes, until risen. Preheat the oven to 400°F (200°C).

18 Let the pastries cool slighty, then move to a wire rack.

17 Brush with egg and bake for 15–20 minutes, until golden.

Top tip

The pastries will keep in an airtight container for up to two days.

Apple jalousie

In France, a *jalousie* is a type of window shutter. The top of this delicious pastry is sliced to look like a shutter, showing the apple inside.

TRY THIS

If you want to make this with a different fruit, then replace the same quantity of apples for peeled, cored, and diced pears.

Level rating

How long?   1½ hrs prep, 1 hr 15 mins chilling, 40 mins baking

How many?   6–8

Ingredients

18 tbsp unsalted butter, frozen for 30 minutes

2 cups all-purpose flour, sifted, plus extra for dusting

1 tsp salt

1 tsp lemon juice

For the filling

1 tbsp unsalted butter

2¼lb (1kg) apples, peeled, cored, and diced

1in (2.5cm) piece of ginger, finely chopped

½ cup granulated sugar

1 large egg white, beaten, for glazing

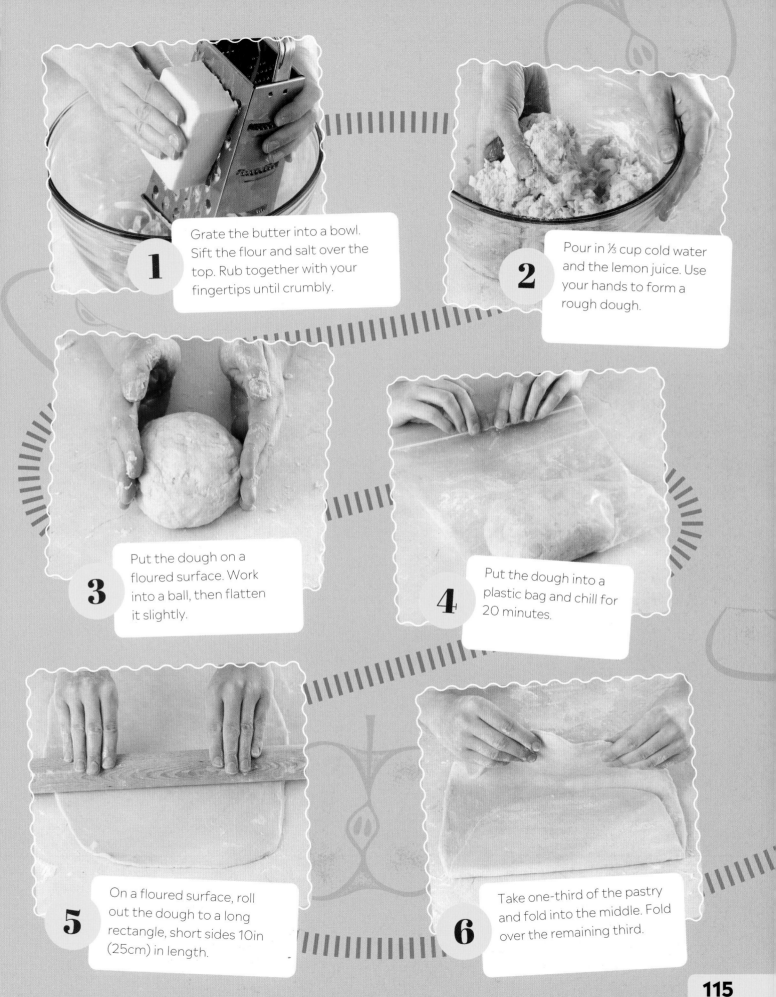

1 Grate the butter into a bowl. Sift the flour and salt over the top. Rub together with your fingertips until crumbly.

2 Pour in ⅓ cup cold water and the lemon juice. Use your hands to form a rough dough.

3 Put the dough on a floured surface. Work into a ball, then flatten it slightly.

4 Put the dough into a plastic bag and chill for 20 minutes.

5 On a floured surface, roll out the dough to a long rectangle, short sides 10in (25cm) in length.

6 Take one-third of the pastry and fold into the middle. Fold over the remaining third.

7 Turn it over so the seams are easily sealed when it is rerolled.

8 Roll in the longer direction to a similar size as the original rectangle. Keep the short sides even in size.

9 Repeat the folding and rolling once more. Return it to the bag and chill for 20 minutes.

10 Roll and fold the pastry twice more, then chill for a final 20 minutes.

11 In a pan, melt the butter. Add the apples, ginger, and all but two tablespoons of the sugar.

12 Fry and stir for 15–20 minutes, until the apples are soft and golden. Leave to cool.

13 Roll out the pastry on a floured surface to 11 x 13in (28 x 32cm). Cut in half to make two 5½ x 13in (14 x 32cm) rectangles.

14 Fold one half lengthwise and cut across the fold at ¼in (5mm) gaps, leaving a border on one side.

15 Put the uncut dough on a nonstick baking sheet and spoon the apple along the center. Brush the edges with a little water.

16 Unfold the cut dough and place on top of the apples. Press the edges to seal together. Chill for 15 minutes. Preheat the oven to 425°F (220°C).

17 Bake for 20–25 minutes. Then brush with the egg white and sprinkle the remaining sugar over the top.

Top tip

To prepare ahead, the jalousie can be frozen at Step 16.

18 Put back in the oven and continue baking for 10–15 minutes. Serve the slices warm or at room temperature.

Cinnamon palmiers

These curly cinnamon-spiced pastries were given their name because of their shape. In French *palmier* means "palm tree." They are super tasty and make a breakfast extra special.

Top tip

The palmiers will keep in an airtight container for up to three days.

Level rating

  🧁🧁🧁

How long?

45 mins prep,
1 hr 10 mins chilling,
30 mins baking

How many?

24

Ingredients

18 tbsp unsalted butter, frozen
   for 30 minutes
2 cups all-purpose flour, plus extra
   for dusting
1 tsp salt
1 large egg, lightly beaten, for glazing

For the filling

7 tbsp unsalted butter, softened
½ cup light brown sugar
4–5 tsp ground cinnamon, to taste

1 Grate the butter into a bowl. Sift the flour and salt over the top. Rub together with your fingertips, until crumbly.

2 Pour in ⅓ cup cold water. Use a fork, then your hands to form a rough dough.

3 Put the dough into a plastic bag and chill for 20 minutes.

4 On a floured surface, thinly roll it out to a long rectangle, short sides 10in (25cm) in length.

5 Take one-third of the pastry and fold into the middle. Fold over the remaining third.

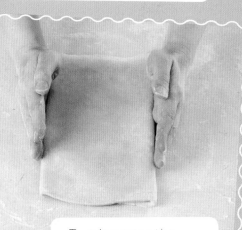

6 Turn it over so the seams are easily sealed when it is rerolled.

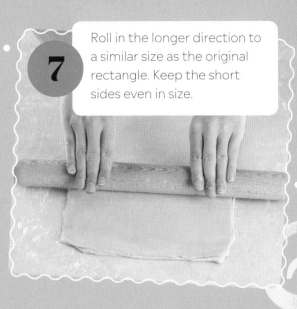

7 Roll in the longer direction to a similar size as the original rectangle. Keep the short sides even in size.

8 Repeat the folding and rolling once more. Put back in the bag and chill for 20 minutes.

9 Roll and fold the pastry twice more, then chill for a final 20 minutes.

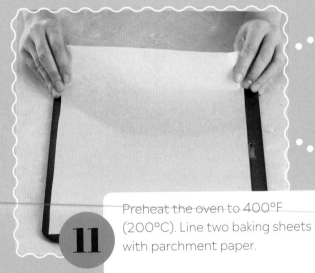

10 Make the filling by beating together the butter, sugar, and cinnamon.

11 Preheat the oven to 400°F (200°C). Line two baking sheets with parchment paper.

12 Roll the dough out once again, so that the long edge measures 19in (48cm). Trim the edges. Spread the filling thinly over the surface.

13 Loosely roll one of the long sides into the middle, and repeat with the other side.

14 Brush with the egg, press together, then turn over and chill for 10 minutes.

15 Carefully cut into 24 pieces, ¾in (2cm) thick. Then turn the palmiers face up.

16 Squeeze them to form an oval, and press down lightly with your palm to flatten slightly. Put on the lined baking sheets.

17 Brush the palmiers with the beaten egg and bake for 25–30 minutes.

18 They are ready when golden brown, puffed up, and crisp in the center. Put on a wire rack to cool before serving.

Simple strudel

This sweet pastry is a traditional European dessert. *Strudel* is German for "whirlpool," because when it is cut open you can see swirls of pastry filled with delicious apples and almonds.

Level rating

How long?   30 mins prep,
                30 mins resting,
                40 mins baking

How many?   6–8

Ingredients

1¼ cups all-purpose flour, plus extra
   for dusting

¼ tsp salt

1 tsp granulated sugar, plus extra for
   sprinkling

7 tbsp unsalted butter, cold and diced,
   plus extra for greasing and brushing

1 large egg, beaten

½ tsp cider vinegar

1 tbsp confectioners' sugar, for dusting

For the filling

2lb (900g) tart apples, such as Granny
   Smith, peeled, cored, and thinly sliced

grated zest of ½ lemon

½ cup bread crumbs

½ cup granulated sugar

3 tbsp dark brown sugar

1 tsp ground cinnamon

¼ tsp grated nutmeg

1½oz (45g) slivered almonds

¼ tsp vanilla extract

1 Combine the flour, salt, and sugar in a large bowl. Rub in two tablespoons of the butter until it looks like bread crumbs. In a separate bowl, beat the egg, vinegar, and ¼ cup cold water. Add the liquid to the dry ingredients and mix to make a loose dough.

2 Knead the dough on a lightly floured work surface for 10–15 minutes, until it is smooth and elastic. Put it in a lightly greased bowl, cover with plastic wrap, and leave to rest for 30 minutes.

3 For the filling, combine the apples, zest, bread crumbs, two types of sugar, cinnamon, nutmeg, almonds, and vanilla in a large bowl. Lightly flour a large, clean dish towel and place the pastry on top.

START at the CENTER and WORK OUTWARD to STRETCH OUT the PASTRY.

4 Roll the pastry into a large rectangle. Gently stretch it out to about 16 x 24in (40 x 61cm), or until it is very thin. Preheat the oven to 375°F (190°C). Line a baking sheet with parchment paper.

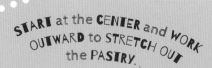

5 Melt the remaining butter in a saucepan over low heat and brush over the pastry. Put the filling at one end of the pastry. Lift the edges of the dish towel and slowly roll up the strudel, working gently but firmly.

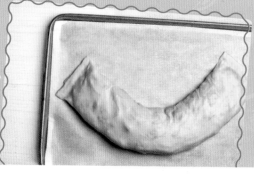

6 Place the strudel on the baking sheet. Curve it into a half circle and brush with melted butter. Sprinkle over some granulated sugar and trim the edges. Bake for 35–40 minutes, until golden. Dust with confectioners' sugar and serve warm.

Fruity crumble pie

Topped with a tasty oat and pecan crumble, this pie is sure to be a hit with your friends. Serve warm with vanilla ice cream, or pair with salted caramel ice cream for an even richer flavor.

Level rating

How long?   25 mins prep,
30 mins chilling,
1 hr 10 mins baking

How many?   8

Ingredients

For the pie crust

1⅔ cups all-purpose flour, plus extra for dusting

7 tbsp unsalted butter, chilled and diced, plus extra for greasing

1 large egg, beaten

For the topping

½ cup all-purpose flour

2 tbsp light brown sugar

½ tsp ground cinnamon

5 tbsp unsalted butter, softened and diced

½ cup rolled oats

1½oz (45g) chopped pecans

For the filling

9oz (250g) blueberries

9oz (250g) apples, peeled, cored, and diced into ½in (1cm) cubes

2 tbsp cornstarch

3 tbsp granulated sugar

Special equipment

9in (23cm) deep-sided, loose-bottomed fluted tart pan

baking beans

1 Put the flour in a bowl and rub in the butter until it looks like bread crumbs. Mix in the egg to form a smooth dough. Wrap in plastic wrap and chill for 30 minutes. Preheat the oven to 350°F (180°C). Grease the pan.

2 On a floured surface, roll the pie crust into a circle, ¼in (5mm) thick, and use it to line the pan. Trim the excess crust, prick the bottom, and line with parchment paper. Fill with baking beans, place on a baking sheet and bake for 20 minutes. Take out the beans and paper and bake for another five minutes. Remove and let cool.

3 Increase the oven temperature to 375°F (190°C). For the topping, mix together the flour, sugar, and cinnamon. Rub the butter into the mixture. Stir in the oats and pecans.

4 For the filling, put the blueberries, apples, cornstarch, and sugar in a bowl. Stir to coat the fruit.

Top tip

The apple cubes should be small enough to cook through while baking but not lose their texture.

5 Spread the filling evenly in the pie crust and pack it down slightly. Then put the topping on the filling and spread it out loosely and evenly.

6 Bake for 40–45 minutes. Cover with foil if it browns too quickly. Cool for 30 minutes. Take out of the pan and serve immediately.

Sweet cherry pie

This pie is an American classic. The fresh cherries and buttery pastry go together perfectly. It is best served warm, with a scoop of vanilla ice cream.

Level rating

How long? 35 mins prep,
50 mins chilling,
1 hr 5 mins baking

How many? 8

Ingredients

1½ cups all-purpose flour, plus
extra for dusting

1 tsp salt

2 tbsp granulated sugar

16 tbsp unsalted butter, chilled
and diced

2 tsp apple cider vinegar

For the filling

¼ cup granulated sugar, plus extra
for sprinkling

¼ cup cornstarch

1 tbsp lemon juice

grated zest of ½ lemon

pinch of salt

½ tsp vanilla extract

2lb (900g) sweet cherries, pitted

1 tbsp unsalted butter, chilled
and diced

1 large egg, lightly beaten, to glaze

Special equipment

9in (23cm) round pie pan,
about 2in (5cm) deep

1 Put the flour, salt, and sugar in a large bowl and mix well. Rub in the butter until it looks like bread crumbs. In a separate bowl, mix the vinegar with ⅔ cup cold water.

2 Slowly add the vinegar mix to the dry ingredients, using two forks to fluff and stir, until well combined.

3 On a lightly floured surface, bring the mixture together to form a loose dough. Knead gently for 4–5 minutes, until soft.

4 Cut off one-third of the dough. Wrap the two portions of dough in plastic wrap and chill for 30 minutes. Grease the pie pan.

5 On a floured surface, roll out the larger portion of the pie dough to a 12–13in (30–33cm) circle, about ⅛in (3mm) thick. Use it to line the pie pan, leaving a ¾in (2cm) overhang.

6 For the filling, put the sugar, cornstarch, lemon juice, zest, salt, and vanilla in a large bowl and stir to combine. Mix in the cherries and leave to soften for 10–15 minutes.

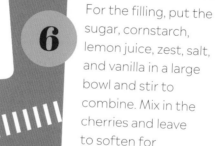

7 Pour the filling into the pie crust and add the butter. Roll out the small portion of pie dough to just larger than the pie. Place it on top of the filling and pinch the edges together. Chill in the freezer for 15–20 minutes. Preheat the oven to 400°F (200°C).

8 Brush the top with the beaten egg and sprinkle the sugar on top. Cut four slits on top of the pie. Bake for 35–45 minutes, then reduce the temperature to 350°F (180°C). Bake for another 15–20 minutes, until golden.

Pumpkin pie

Dark, rich, and sweet, this traditional Thanksgiving pie has all the fragrance and flavors of fall wrapped in a crisp pie crust. Serve it with a dollop of whipped cream or a scoop of ice cream.

Level rating

How long?   40 mins prep,
1 hr 25 mins baking,
1 hr chilling

How many?   8

Ingredients

8 tbsp unsalted butter, chilled and diced, plus extra for greasing

1 cup all-purpose flour, plus extra for dusting

1 tbsp granulated sugar

½ tsp salt

1 tsp apple juice

whipped cream, to serve

For the filling

14oz (400g) can pumpkin puree

½ cup whole milk

1 cup dark brown sugar

1⅛ tsp ground cinnamon

½ tsp grated nutmeg

⅛ tsp ground pumpkin pie spice

½ tsp salt

2 large eggs

Special equipment

9in (23cm) pie pan, about 2in (5cm) deep

baking beans

1 Grease the pie pan. Mix the flour, sugar, and salt in a bowl. Rub in the butter until the mixture looks like bread crumbs. In another bowl, mix the apple juice with ½ cup cold water.

2 Slowly add ¼ cup of the liquid mix to the flour mix. Use two forks to stir them together until clumps form.

3 On a lightly floured surface, gently knead the mixture until it forms a dough. Wrap in plastic wrap and chill for 30 minutes. Grease the pie pan.

4 On a floured surface, roll out the pie crust to a 12in (30cm) circle, ⅛in (2mm) thick. Line the pie pan, leaving a ½in (1cm) overhang. Use your fingers to crimp (pinch) the top of the pie all the way around the edge. Chill for 30 minutes.

5

Preheat the oven to 375°F (190°C).

6

Prick the bottom of the pie crust with a fork. Line it with parchment paper and fill with baking beans. Place on a baking sheet. Bake for 25 minutes, until lightly brown at the edges.

7

Take out the beans and paper. Bake for 6–10 minutes, until golden. Leave to cool on a wire rack. Reduce the oven temperature to 350°F (180°C).

8

Whisk the pumpkin puree, milk, and brown sugar until smooth. Beat in the spices, salt, and eggs until well mixed.

9

Pour the filling into the pie crust and place on a baking sheet. Cover the edges with foil. Bake for 35–40 minutes. Remove the foil and bake for 10 minutes, until set. Serve warm.

Ultimate apple pie

This recipe is one to bake when it's really cold outside. It's a comfort food that all your family and friends will enjoy.

TRY THIS

To make an apple and blackberry pie, add 9oz (250g) blackberries at Step 8 and gently mix together with the apples.

Level rating 🧁🧁🧁

How long?
35 mins prep,
1 hr 15 mins chilling,
55 mins baking

How many?   6–8

Ingredients

2 cups all-purpose flour, plus extra for dusting

½ tsp salt

11 tbsp lard or vegetable shortening, cubed, plus extra for greasing

2 tbsp granulated sugar, plus extra for sprinkling

1 tbsp milk, for glazing

For the filling

2¼lb (1kg) apples, peeled, cored, and sliced

juice of 1 lemon

2 tbsp all-purpose flour

½ tsp ground cinnamon

¼ tsp grated nutmeg

½ cup granulated sugar

Special equipment

9in (23cm) shallow pie pan

1 Sift the flour and salt into a bowl. Add the lard or vegetable shortening and cut across it with two butter knives.

2 Using your fingertips, rub the lard or vegetable shortening into the flour until crumbs form. Lift the mixture to add air to it.

3 Add the sugar. Sprinkle with 6–7 tablespoons of cold water. Mix together with a fork.

4 Press the crumbs into a ball, wrap in plastic wrap, and chill for 30 minutes. Grease the pan with lard or vegetable shortening.

5 On a floured surface, roll two-thirds of the dough out to a round 2in (5cm) larger than the pan.

6 Using the rolling pin, drape the pie dough over the pan and gently push it down.

7 Using a sharp knife, carefully trim any excess pie dough, then chill for 15 minutes, until firm.

8 Put the apple slices in a bowl and pour the lemon juice over the top. Mix to coat the apples in juice.

9 Sprinkle the flour, cinnamon, nutmeg, and sugar over the top of the apples. Mix to coat the apples.

10 Put the apples in the pie pan and use a pastry brush to brush the edge of the pie dough with water. Roll the rest of the dough to an 11in (28cm) round.

11 Wrap the pie dough around the rolling pin and drape it over the filling. Carefully trim the overhang.

12 Press the edges together to seal, carefully crimping with the back of a knife as you go.

13 Carefully cut an "X" in the top crust. Gently pull back the point of each triangle to reveal the filling.

14 Roll out the trimmings, cut into strips, and moisten with a little water. Lay on the pie in a crisscross pattern. Brush the milk over the pie.

15 Sprinkle sugar on top. Chill for 30 minutes. Preheat the oven to 425°F (220°C). Bake for 20 minutes.

16 Reduce the oven temperature to 350°F (180°C). Bake for another 30–35 minutes. Insert a skewer to check that the apples are tender. Serve warm.

Very berry plum pie

Berries and plums give this fruity pie a deliciously sweet flavor. It goes perfectly with a scoop of ice cream!

Level rating

How long?   15 mins prep,
30 mins chilling,
30 mins baking

How many?   6–8

Ingredients

all-purpose flour, for dusting

1lb 2oz (500g) store-bought puff pastry

1 large egg, beaten

1lb 6oz (650g) mixed berries—raspberries and strawberries

2 tbsp granulated sugar

2 tbsp cornstarch

7oz (200g) plums, pitted and cut into quarters

1 On a lightly floured surface, roll out the puff pastry until it's about ¼in (5mm) thick.

2 Put a 10in (25cm) plate on the pastry and carefully cut around it with a knife. Move the circle onto a baking sheet and brush a little beaten egg all over the surface.

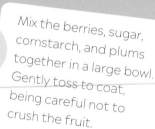

3 Mix the berries, sugar, cornstarch, and plums together in a large bowl. Gently toss to coat, being careful not to crush the fruit.

4 Spoon the fruit into the middle of the pastry, leaving a 3in (7.5cm) border around the outside.

6 Brush the pastry with the remaining beaten egg. Bake for 30 minutes, until golden brown, rotating halfway through baking. Leave to cool for 30 minutes, then serve.

5 Scrunch up the edges and bring them toward the center, leaving the middle uncovered. Chill in the fridge for 30 minutes. Preheat the oven to 400°F (200°C).

SWEET BERRIES

TRY THIS

Other fruits, such as blueberries, peaches, apples, blackberries, and pears will also taste great in this recipe.

Key lime pie

This dessert is named after the small limes that grow in the Florida Keys, where the recipe comes from. The zesty limes give the pie a delicious pop of flavor!

1 Preheat the oven to 350°F (180°C).

2 Pulse the graham crackers in a food processor to a fine powder and put in a bowl. Add the butter and mix well to combine.

3 Spread the mixture in the pie pan, pressing it evenly into the bottom and sides for a firm crust. Bake for 8–10 minutes, until golden. Set aside to cool.

4 Beat the egg, yolk, and zest in a bowl for two minutes. Then beat in the milk, lime juice, and salt until smooth. Pour over the crust. Bake for 25–30 minutes, until the filling is set.

5 Leave to cool completely. Chill for two hours. For the topping, beat the cream and sugar in a bowl to form stiff peaks. Spread it over the pie. Decorate with lime zest.

Level rating 🧁

How long?   15 mins prep,
40 mins baking,
2 hrs chilling

How many?   8

Ingredients

6oz (175g) graham crackers, crushed
5 tbsp unsalted butter, melted

For the filling

1 large egg, plus 1 yolk
1 tbsp grated lime zest, plus extra to decorate
14oz (400g) can condensed milk
1 cup lime juice
pinch of salt

For the topping

¾ cup heavy cream
2 tsp confectioners' sugar

Special equipment

9in (23cm) round pie pan, about 2in (5cm) deep

ZINGY AND CREAMY

Top tip

You can store the baked crust in an airtight container in the fridge up to one day ahead of serving.

Raspberry crème tartlets

These tartlets look stunning and are incredibly simple to make. The pie crusts and crème pâtissière are easy to make ahead, so you can assemble the tarts at the last minute.

Ingredients

1 cup all-purpose flour, plus extra for dusting
2 tbsp granulated sugar
7 tbsp unsalted butter, chilled and diced
1 large egg, beaten with 1 tbsp ice water

For the crème pâtissière

1 cup + 1 tbsp whole milk
2 large egg yolks
¼ cup granulated sugar
2 tbsp cornstarch
1 tsp vanilla extract

For the topping

3 tbsp apricot jam, strained
9oz (250g) raspberries

Special equipment

4 x 4in (10cm) loose-bottomed fluted pie pans
baking beans

Top tip

To prepare ahead, store the crème pâtissière in an airtight container in the fridge for up to two days. Wrap and store the pie crusts in the fridge for up to three days.

1 Mix the flour and sugar in a bowl, then rub in the butter to form crumbs. Mix in the egg to make a dough. Add more ice water if it's dry. Knead briefly and wrap in plastic wrap. Chill for 30 minutes.

Trim any EXCESS DOUGH.

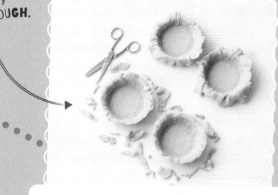

2 Preheat the oven to 350°F (180°C). Divide the pie crust into four. On a floured surface, roll out each portion to a circle, ⅛in (3mm) thick, and use to line the pans, leaving an overhang of ½in (1cm).

3 Prick the crusts using a fork, line with parchment paper, and fill with baking beans. Bake on a baking sheet for 15 minutes. Take out the beans and parchment, and bake for 5–10 minutes. Trim the overhang. Cool completely before taking the crusts out of the pans.

4 To make the crème, heat the milk until hot, but not boiling. In a small bowl, whisk the egg yolks, sugar, cornstarch, and vanilla, and slowly pour in the hot milk. Put in a saucepan.

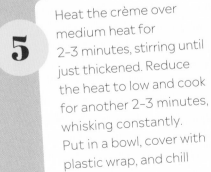

5 Heat the crème over medium heat for 2–3 minutes, stirring until just thickened. Reduce the heat to low and cook for another 2–3 minutes, whisking constantly. Put in a bowl, cover with plastic wrap, and chill until cold.

6 Heat the jam and one tablespoon of water over low heat, stirring until smooth. Take off the heat and let it cool. Spoon the crème pâtissière into the crusts. Put the raspberries on top. Add a little apricot glaze. Chill for one hour before serving.

Three ways
with tartlets

These tasty little treats are packed with flavor and are a perfect dessert if you're having friends over. They all taste amazing, and they're great served with a bowl of fresh strawberries.

Custard tartlets

Ingredients

2 tbsp unsalted butter
3 sheets phyllo dough
flour, for dusting

For the filling
1 cup whole milk
⅔ cup heavy cream
6 cardamom pods, crushed
2 large eggs, whisked
2 tbsp granulated sugar

Special equipment
deep 6-hole, 2½in- (6cm-) wide muffin pan,
    greased

1 Preheat the oven to 375°F (190°C).

2 Heat the milk, cream, and cardamom pods in a heavy-bottomed saucepan until steaming. Take off the heat.

3 Melt the butter in a separate saucepan over medium heat.

4 On a floured surface, spread out one phyllo dough sheet and brush it with a little of the melted butter.

5 Cover with another phyllo sheet, brush with butter, and top with the final phyllo sheet. Cut the dough into six equal pieces.

6 Line the pan with the phyllo, allowing the edges to stick up over the rim. Brush the edges with butter. Cover with a damp paper towel.

7 Combine the eggs and sugar in a bowl. Pour the milk through a sieve into the egg mixture. Whisk the custard, transfer to a pitcher, and pour evenly into the phyllo shells.

8 Bake for 15–20 minutes. Cool in the pan for 10 minutes, then remove.

Banana and chocolate tartlets

Ingredients

1¼ cups all-purpose flour
2 tbsp granulated sugar
7 tbsp unsalted butter, chilled
1 large egg yolk

For the filling and topping
¼oz (10g) sweetened flaked coconut
2 tbsp all-purpose flour
2 tbsp light brown sugar
2 tbsp unsalted butter, softened
2–3 bananas, cut into ½in (1cm) slices
6 tbsp chocolate spread

Special equipment
6 x 4in (10cm) loose-bottomed tart pans
baking beans

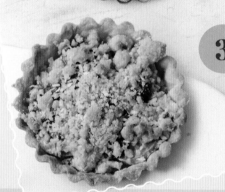

1 Follow the instructions for Steps 1–3 on page 139. Then, increase the oven temperature to 400°F (200°C).

2 In a bowl, combine the coconut, flour, and brown sugar. Rub in the butter until the mixture looks like bread crumbs.

3 Line each crust with banana slices and one tablespoon of chocolate spread. Sprinkle the coconut topping over the top.

4 Bake for 15 minutes. Leave to cool in the pans, then remove and serve.

Mocha tartlets

Ingredients

¾ cup all-purpose flour
2 tbsp granulated sugar
¼ cup cocoa powder
7 tbsp unsalted butter, chilled and diced
3 tbsp cooled strong black coffee

For the filling
1¼ cups heavy cream
9oz (250g) bittersweet chocolate, chopped
2 large eggs
1 tsp vanilla extract

Special equipment
6 x 4in (10cm) loose-bottomed tart pans
baking beans

1 Combine the flour, sugar, and cocoa in a bowl. Rub in the butter until the mixture looks like bread crumbs.

2 Add the coffee. Bring together to form a dough. Knead it briefly until smooth, wrap in plastic wrap, and chill for 30 minutes.

3 Follow Steps 2 and 3 on page 139. Then reduce the oven temperature to 325°F (160°C).

4 Heat the heavy cream in a heavy-bottomed saucepan until steaming. Remove and stir in the chocolate until melted. Beat until smooth, move to a bowl, and leave to cool.

5 Gradually whisk in the eggs and stir in the vanilla. Pour the filling into the crusts.

6 Bake for 20 minutes. Leave to cool in the pans. Then remove and serve immediately.

Tangy lemon tart

This French tart, known as "tarte au citron," is filled to the brim with mouthwatering lemony custard. Serve this delicious dessert with single cream and raspberries.

Level rating

How long?   20 mins prep,
                  1 hr chilling,
                  1 hr 10 mins baking

How many?   8

Ingredients

1⅔ cups all-purpose flour, plus extra
    for dusting
2 tbsp granulated sugar
7 tbsp unsalted butter,
    chilled and diced
1 large egg, beaten
light cream, to serve
raspberries, to serve

For the filling

¾ cup heavy cream
¾ cup granulated sugar
grated zest and juice of 2 lemons
4 large eggs, plus 1 egg yolk

Special equipment

9in (23cm) loose-bottomed fluted pie pan
baking beans

1 Mix the flour and sugar in a bowl. Then rub in the butter to form crumbs. Stir in the egg to form a dough. Add a little iced water if dry. Knead briefly on a floured surface, until smooth. Wrap in plastic wrap and chill for one hour.

2 Preheat the oven to 350°F (180°C). On a floured surface, roll out the pastry to a large circle, ⅛in (3mm) thick. Use it to line the pan, leaving an overhang of ¾in (2cm). Knead the pastry briefly if it crumbles. Prick the pastry, line with parchment paper, and fill with baking beans.

3 Place on a baking sheet and bake for 20–25 minutes. Remove the beans and parchment paper and bake for another five minutes, until golden. Trim the pastry. For the filling, whisk all the ingredients in a bowl until well combined.

4 Pour the filling into the crust. Bake on a baking sheet for 40–45 minutes, until just set. Take out of the pan and cool to room temperature before serving.

Top tip

You can store the tart crust in an airtight container for up to three days ahead of serving.

Chocolate pie

With its deliciously rich filling, this pie is perfect for chocoholics. It can be served warm or cold and goes perfectly with fresh raspberries.

TRY THIS

For a tangy twist, spread ¼ cup of orange marmalade on the pie crust while it is still warm.

Level rating

How long? 30 mins prep, 1 hr chilling, 40 mins baking

How many? 8–10

Ingredients

1¼ cups all-purpose flour, plus extra for dusting
7 tbsp unsalted butter, chilled and diced
¼ cup granulated sugar
1 large egg yolk
½ tsp vanilla extract
raspberries, to serve

For the filling

11 tbsp unsalted butter, diced
7oz (200g) bittersweet chocolate, broken into pieces
3 large eggs
2 tbsp granulated sugar
½ cup heavy cream

Special equipment

9in (22cm) loose-bottomed fluted pie pan
baking beans

1 In a large bowl, rub the flour and butter together until fine crumbs form.

2 Add the sugar to the crumb mixture and stir to combine.

3 Beat the egg yolk with the vanilla, then add them to the crumb mixture.

4 Bring it together to form a dough. Add a little cold water if it is dry. Wrap in plastic wrap and chill for one hour.

5 Preheat the oven to 350°F (180°C). On a floured surface, roll out the pie dough to a circle, ⅛in (3mm) thick.

6 If the pie crust begins to crumble, bring it together with your hands and knead gently. Then roll it out again.

7 Use it to line the pie pan, leaving an overlapping edge of ¾in (2cm). With a pair of scissors, carefully trim any excess dough that hangs down farther than this.

8 Prick the pie crust all over with a fork to prevent air bubbles from forming during baking.

9 Line the pie crust with parchment paper. Scatter baking beans over and put the pan on a baking sheet. Bake for 20 minutes.

Top tip

The pie will keep in the fridge for up to two days.

10 Remove the beans and parchment paper. Bake for five minutes more. Trim any excess pie dough.

11 Melt the butter and chocolate in a heatproof bowl over a pan of simmering water, stirring. Set aside to cool.

12 Whisk together the eggs and granulated sugar in a bowl until well blended.

13 Pour in the cooled chocolate mixture and whisk gently until well combined.

14 Mix in the heavy cream. Pour the chocolate mixture into a liquid measuring cup.

15 Keeping the pie crust on the baking sheet, pour the filling into the pie crust and smooth the top.

16 Bake for 10–15 minutes, until just set. Leave to cool for five minutes, then remove from the pan and place on a serving platter.

Pinwheel pear tart

A rich, buttery crust makes this French tart irresistible. The combination of pears and frangipane (a sweet almond paste) is absolutely delicious. You can use apples instead of pears, if you prefer.

Level rating

How long?
30 mins prep,
45 mins chilling,
45 mins baking

How many?   8

Ingredients

5 tbsp unsalted butter, softened
    and diced, plus extra for greasing
1¼ cups all-purpose flour, sifted, plus
    extra for dusting
3 large egg yolks
¼ cup granulated sugar
pinch of salt
½ tsp vanilla extract
3–4 ripe pears, peeled, cored,
    and cut into wedges
juice of 1 lemon
heavy cream, to serve

For the frangipane

9 tbsp unsalted butter, softened
½ cup granulated sugar
1 large egg, plus 1 large egg yolk,
    lightly beaten
1 cup ground almonds
2 tbsp all-purpose flour, sifted

For the glaze

5½oz (150g) apricot jam

Special equipment

9in (23cm) loose-bottomed,
    fluted pie pan

1 Grease the pie pan. Put the flour in a large bowl and make a well in the center. Put the butter, egg yolks, sugar, salt, and vanilla extract in the well and mix to combine.

2 Use your fingertips to bring the mix together and make a sticky dough. Add cold water if needed. Lightly knead the dough on a floured surface for 1–2 minutes. Wrap in plastic wrap. Chill for 30 minutes.

3 On a floured surface, roll out the pie crust to an 11in (28cm) circle. Line the pan and trim any overhang. Prick the bottom with a fork and chill for 15 minutes.

4

Preheat the oven to 400°F (200°C).

5

For the frangipane, beat the butter and sugar in a large bowl for 2–3 minutes, until fluffy. Beat in the egg and yolk, a little at a time. Stir in one tablespoon of water, the ground almonds, and flour.

6

Coat the pears with the lemon juice in a small bowl. Spread the frangipane evenly in the pie crust and top with the pears in a spiral pattern. Put the pan on a baking sheet and bake for 12–15 minutes. Reduce the heat to 350°F (180°C). Bake for another 25–30 minutes, until the filling is set.

7

Cool slightly, then take out of the pan. For the glaze, push the jam through a sieve into a heatproof bowl. Add 2–3 tablespoons of water, melt over a saucepan of hot water, and brush over the tart. Serve warm, with heavy cream.

Top tip

You can prepare and store the pie crust in an airtight container in the fridge for up to three days ahead of serving.

Almond and raspberry lattice tart

Pie crust is easy to make patterns with, and it creates an impressive dessert. In this recipe it's used to make a crisscross design.

Ingredients

¾ cup all-purpose flour,
   plus extra for dusting
pinch of ground cloves
½ tsp ground cinnamon
1½ cups ground almonds
9 tbsp unsalted butter, softened
   and diced, plus extra for greasing
1 large egg yolk
½ cup granulated sugar
¼ tsp salt
finely grated zest of 1 lemon and juice
   of ½ lemon

For the filling

½ cup granulated sugar
13oz (375g) raspberries
1–2 tbsp confectioners' sugar, for dusting

Special equipment

9in (23cm) loose-bottomed fluted pie pan
fluted pastry wheel (optional)

1 Sift the flour into a bowl. Mix in the cloves, cinnamon, and almonds, and make a well.

2 Using your fingers, mix the butter, yolk, sugar, salt, zest, and juice in a separate bowl. Place in the well.

3 Mix in the flour with your fingers and work it until coarse crumbs form. Form the dough into a ball.

4 Knead the dough for 1–2 minutes, until smooth. Wrap in plastic wrap. Chill for 1–2 hours.

5 Cook the granulated sugar and raspberries in a pan for 10–12 minutes, until thick. Leave to cool.

6 With the back of a wooden spoon, press half of the fruit pulp through a sieve.

7 Stir in the remaining pulp from the pan. Grease the pan and preheat the oven to 375°F (190°C).

8 Flour the work surface. Roll out two-thirds of the dough into an 11in (28cm) round.

9 Use the dough to line the pan and cut off any excess overhang.

Top tip

The tart can be stored in an airtight container for up to two days.

10 Spread the filling in the crust. Roll the rest of the dough to a 6 x 12in (15 x 30cm) rectangle.

11 Using a fluted wheel, for a decorative edge, cut the dough into 5 x ½in (12 x 1cm) strips.

12 Arrange half the strips from left to right over the top, ¾in (2cm) apart.

13 Put the other strips diagonally over the top. Trim the overhang, roll out the trimmings, and cut four strips.

14 Brush the edge of the pastry with water and attach the edge strips. Chill for 15 minutes.

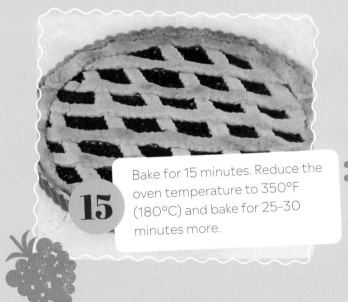

15 Bake for 15 minutes. Reduce the oven temperature to 350°F (180°C) and bake for 25–30 minutes more.

16 Leave to cool, then remove from the pan and, about 30 minutes before serving, lightly dust with confectioners' sugar.

Strawberry tart

This gorgeous tart tastes as good as it looks. Finished with a jelly glaze, it will look as if it were made by a professional pastry chef!

Top tip

The tart is best eaten on the day it's made, but will keep chilled overnight.

Ingredients

1 cup all-purpose flour, plus extra
for dusting

7 tbsp unsalted butter, chilled
and diced

¼ cup granulated sugar

1 large egg yolk

½ tsp vanilla extract

6 tbsp red currant jelly, for glazing

10oz (300g) strawberries, hulled, washed,
and sliced into thick slices

For the crème pâtissière

½ cup granulated sugar

½ cup cornstarch

2 large eggs

1 tsp vanilla extract

1¾ cups whole milk

Special equipment

9in (22cm) loose-bottomed fluted pie pan
baking beans

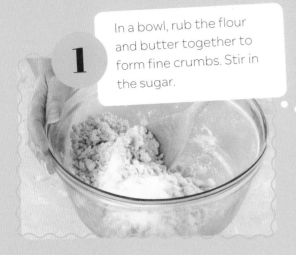

1 In a bowl, rub the flour and butter together to form fine crumbs. Stir in the sugar.

2 Beat together the egg yolk and vanilla extract and add to the flour mixture.

3 Bring together to form a dough. Add a little water if dry. Wrap in plastic wrap and chill for one hour.

4 Preheat the oven to 350°F (180°C). Roll out the pie crust to a thickness of ⅛in (3mm).

5 If the crust starts to crumble, bring it together with your hands and gently knead.

6 Use the rolled-out pie crust to line the pan, leaving an overlapping edge of ¾in (2cm) around the pan.

7 Use a pair of scissors or a knife to trim any excess pie crust that hangs down farther than ¾in (2cm).

8 Prick the crust bottom all over with a fork, to prevent air bubbles from forming as it bakes.

9 Carefully line the pie crust with a piece of parchment paper.

10 Scatter the baking beans over the parchment paper. Put on a baking sheet and bake for 20 minutes.

11 Take out the beans and parchment paper, and bake for five minutes more. Carefully trim any excess crust with a knife.

12 Melt the jelly with one tablespoon of water and brush a little over the pie crust. Leave to cool.

13 For the crème pâtissière, beat the sugar, cornstarch, eggs, and vanilla extract in a bowl.

14 In a heavy-bottomed saucepan, bring the milk to a boil and take it off the heat just as it bubbles.

15 Pour the hot milk onto the egg mixture, whisking all the time.

16 Put the mixture back in the pan and bring to a boil over medium heat, whisking continuously.

17 When the crème thickens, reduce the heat to low and continue to cook for 2-3 minutes, still whisking.

18 Move to a bowl, cover with plastic wrap, and leave it to cool completely.

19 Beat the crème pâtissière and spread it over the pie crust. Top with the strawberries, arranging them in circles.

20 Heat the rest of the jelly glaze again and brush it over the strawberries, then leave to set.

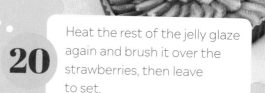

21 Remove from the pan to serve.

Apple crumble

Crumble is a traditional English dessert and it tastes great served with cream, ice cream, or custard.

Level rating

How long? 20 mins prep, 40 mins baking

How many? 6–8

Ingredients

2 tbsp butter, cubed
2lb (900g) Granny Smith apples, peeled, cored, and sliced into wedges
¼ cup brown sugar
2 tbsp apple juice

For the topping

½ cup all-purpose flour
5 tbsp butter, cubed
1½ cups jumbo rolled oats
¼ cup brown sugar
¼ cup mixed seeds, such as sunflower and pumpkin
1 tsp ground cinnamon
heavy cream, ice cream, or custard, to serve

Special equipment

1 quart (1 liter) baking dish

1 Preheat the oven to 350°F (180°C).

2 Melt the butter in a pan and stir in the apples, sugar, and apple juice.

3 Cook for 5–6 minutes, covered, then spoon the apple mixture into the baking dish.

4 For the topping, put the flour in a bowl and rub in the butter with your fingertips until the mixture looks like bread crumbs. Stir in the oats, sugar, seeds, and cinnamon.

5 Spoon the mixture evenly over the top of the apples. Bake for 30–40 minutes, until the topping is golden. Serve warm.

Three ways
with crumble

Follow the instructions on pages 158–159 to make the crumbly topping for all of these delicious crumbles. Try out your own variations, such as swapping the oats for the same amount of all-purpose flour, for a smoother crumble.

Level rating

How long?
20 mins prep,
50 mins baking (Fall fruits),
40 mins baking (Cherry, Plum)

How many?
6–8

Fall fruits crumble

Ingredients

2oz (60g) walnuts
½ tsp ground cinnamon
2 heaping tbsp light brown sugar
4–5 apples, peeled, cored, and cut into cubes
2–3 pears, peeled, cored, and cut into cubes
3½oz (100g) cranberries
1 heaping tbsp all-purpose flour
crumble topping (see pages 158–159)
heavy cream or ice cream, to serve

Serve with CREAM or ICE CREAM.

1 Preheat the oven to 350°F (180°C). Bake the walnuts for five minutes on a baking sheet. Leave to cool, then chop into small pieces.

2 Mix the walnuts, cinnamon, sugar, fruit, and flour together in a baking dish.

3 Pack it all down gently and then sprinkle the crumble topping evenly over the fruit filling. Bake for 45–50 minutes. Serve warm.

Cherry crumble

Ingredients

1¼lb (550g) pitted cherries
2 tbsp granulated sugar
2 tbsp apple juice
crumble topping (see pages 158–159)
custard, to serve

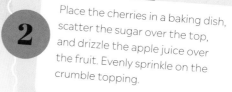

1 Preheat the oven to 350°F (180°C).

2 Place the cherries in a baking dish, scatter the sugar over the top, and drizzle the apple juice over the fruit. Evenly sprinkle on the crumble topping.

3 Bake for 35–40 minutes, or until golden brown. Serve warm.

Plum crumble

Ingredients

1lb 5oz (600g) plums, pitted and halved
2 tbsp maple syrup or honey, to drizzle
crumble topping (see pages 158–159)
custard, to serve

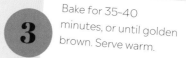

Serve with **CUSTARD.**

TRY THIS

For the topping, swap the all-purpose flour for whole-wheat flour to give the crumble a nuttier flavor.

1 Preheat the oven to 350°F (180°C).

2 Place the plums in a baking dish, drizzle the maple syrup or honey over the top, and sprinkle the crumble topping over evenly.

3 Bake for 30–40 minutes, or until the top is golden brown and the plum juices are bubbling. Serve warm.

Tomato and onion tarts

When baked, puff pastry rises and leaves air pockets inside, making it light and fluffy. Although light, these tarts are surprisingly filling.

Level rating

How long?   10 mins prep,
20 mins baking

How many?   6

Ingredients

all-purpose flour, for dusting
13oz (375g) store-bought puff pastry
oil, for greasing
9oz (250g) cherry tomatoes
9oz (250g) ricotta cheese
2 large eggs, beaten
2 tbsp freshly chopped basil
1oz (25g) Parmesan or mozzarella
   cheese, grated
salt and freshly ground black pepper
1 red onion, sliced
basil leaves, to garnish

TRY THIS

To make this a sweet tart, swap the tomatoes for strawberries and the cheese with chocolate. Take out the red onion, seasoning, and fresh basil.

1

Preheat the oven to 400°F (200°C).

2

On a lightly floured surface, roll out the pastry into a rectangle measuring 10 x 15in (25 x 38cm).

3

Use a knife to cut six equal squares of pastry, then score a ½in (1cm) border around the edges. Move the squares onto a greased baking sheet.

4

Carefully slice the cherry tomatoes in half, using a sharp knife.

5

In a large mixing bowl, mix the ricotta, eggs, basil, and Parmesan cheese. Season with salt and pepper.

6

Spread the mixture on the squares, making sure to stay inside the borders. Scatter the tomatoes and red onion on top and bake for 20 minutes, or until golden. Sprinkle the basil leaves over the tarts before serving.

Mini spinach and phyllo tarts

These simple and light tarts are easy to make and perfect for an afternoon snack or a birthday party. Phyllo dough is tricky to make from scratch, so buy it ready-made.

Level rating

How long?   15 mins prep,
                 25 mins baking

How many?   8

Ingredients

1 tbsp olive oil, plus extra for greasing

9oz (250g) baby spinach leaves, washed

2 tbsp fresh basil

9oz (250g) cream cheese

1 medium egg, beaten

1oz (25g) Cheddar or Parmesan cheese, grated

salt and freshly ground black pepper

9oz (250g) phyllo dough

Special equipment

2 x 6-hole or 1 x 12-hole muffin pans

1 Preheat the oven to 350°F (180°C). Brush the muffin pans with oil and set aside. Tear the spinach and the basil leaves into pieces.

2 In a large mixing bowl, beat the cream cheese, egg, and grated cheese until smooth. Season with salt and pepper, then stir in the spinach and basil.

3 Carefully cut the phyllo dough into 16 squares measuring 5in (12.5cm) each. Brush the squares with a little olive oil.

TRY THIS

To make this into a meaty version, sprinkle 1¾oz (50g) cooked and chopped bacon over the tops of the tarts before baking.

CREAMY AND CRISPY

4

Place one square on top of another phyllo square at an angle to create a star shape. Repeat this process with the rest of the phyllo sheets to make eight tarts.

5

Gently place the phyllo sheets in the muffin pans. Push them into the corners to make them fit.

6

Spoon the mixture into the liners and smooth it down with the back of the spoon. Bake the tarts for 25 minutes, until the filling has set. Serve warm.

Veggie cheese quiche

This savory pie is packed with a delicious creamy filling and is perfect for lunch or a picnic. If you can't find Swiss chard, use spinach instead.

Level rating

How long? 30 mins prep,
1 hr chilling,
1 hr 10 mins baking

How many? 6-8

Ingredients

1¼ cups all-purpose flour, plus
extra for dusting
5 tbsp unsalted butter, chilled
and diced
1 large egg yolk

For the filling

1 tbsp olive oil
1 onion, finely chopped
sea salt
2 garlic cloves, finely chopped
few sprigs of fresh rosemary, leaves
picked and finely chopped
9oz (250g) Swiss chard,
coarsely chopped
4½oz (125g) Gruyère cheese, grated
4½oz (125g) feta cheese, cubed
freshly ground black pepper
2 large eggs, lightly beaten
¾ cup heavy cream or whipping cream

Special equipment

9in (22cm) loose-bottomed fluted pie pan
baking beans

1 To make the crust, rub the flour and butter together in a bowl until fine crumbs form.

2 Lightly beat the egg yolk with one tablespoon of cold water.

3 Add the yolk mix to the crumbs and bring together to form a soft dough. Add extra water if the dough is too dry.

4 Wrap the dough in plastic wrap and chill for one hour. Preheat the oven to 350°F (180°C).

5 On a floured work surface, roll the dough out to a large circle, about ⅛in (3mm) thick.

6 Use the rolling pin to lift the pie crust carefully and put it into the pan, leaving a ¾in (2cm) overhang.

7 Gently push the dough into the pan with your fingers. Prick the bottom all over with a fork.

8 Line with parchment paper and fill with baking beans. Put the pie crust on a baking sheet.

9 Bake for 20–25 minutes. Remove the beans and parchment paper. Bake for five more minutes. Leave to cool and carefully trim the edges with a knife.

Top tip

The quiche is best eaten the same day, but can be chilled overnight if baking in advance.

10 Heat the oil in a pan over low heat. Add the onion and a pinch of salt. Fry the onion until soft. Add the garlic and rosemary and cook for a few seconds.

11 Add the Swiss chard to the pan. Stir for about five minutes, until it wilts.

12 Keeping the pie crust on the baking sheet, spoon in the onion and chard mixture.

13 Sprinkle the Gruyère cheese over the top and scatter with the feta. Season well with salt and pepper.

14 Using a fork, mix together the eggs and cream in a liquid measuring cup until well combined. Carefully pour the cream mix over the filling. Bake for 30–40 minutes, until golden.

15 Leave to cool, then remove from the pan and move to a serving dish. Serve warm or at room temperature.

Mighty meat pie

This is wonderful to take on a picnic, served with a crisp green salad.

Level rating

How long? 1 hr prep, 30 mins chilling, 1½ hrs baking

How many? 8–10

Ingredients

4 cups all-purpose flour, plus extra for dusting

2 tsp salt

5 tbsp butter, chilled and diced, plus extra for greasing

5 tbsp lard, chilled and diced

For the filling

9 large eggs

4 skinless, boneless chicken breasts, total weight 1lb 10oz (750g)

13oz (375g) lean boneless pork

finely grated zest of ½ lemon

1 tsp dried thyme

1 tsp dried sage

large pinch of ground nutmeg

pinch of sea salt and freshly ground black pepper

13oz (375g) cooked lean ham

Special equipment

8–9in (20–23cm) springform cake pan

meat grinder or food processor with blade attachment

Top tip

The pie will keep in the fridge for up to three days.

1 Sift the flour and salt into a large bowl. Rub in the butter and lard until fine crumbs form.

2 Make a well in the flour and add ⅔ cup of cold water. Stir the mixture with a knife to form coarse crumbs.

3 Using your hands, form a dough and knead until smooth. Wrap in plastic wrap and chill for 30 minutes.

4 In a pan, put six eggs in water, bring to a boil, and simmer for seven minutes. Drain, cool, and peel the eggshells off.

5 Cut two of the chicken breasts and all of the pork into chunks. Grind or process, but not too finely.

6 Put the ground meats in a large bowl. Add the lemon zest, thyme, sage, nutmeg, salt, and pepper.

7 In a separate bowl, whisk two eggs and add to the ground meats. Beat the filling until it pulls away from the sides of the bowl.

8 Cut the leftover chicken breasts and the ham into ¾in (2cm) cubes, and stir into the filling.

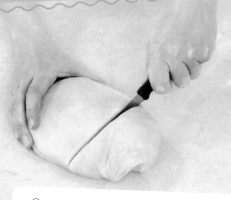

9 Grease the pan. Shape about three-quarters of the dough into a ball. Keep the rest covered with plastic wrap.

10 On a floured surface, roll the dough out to the size of the pan, with a 1in (2.5cm) overhang. Place it in the pan.

11 Preheat the oven to 400°F (200°C). Spoon in half the filling and put the boiled eggs on top.

12 Gently push in the eggs and cover with the remaining mix. Fold over the overhang.

13 Beat the last egg with a pinch of salt, and brush the edges of the pastry with the egg glaze.

14 Roll out the remaining dough to ¼in (5mm) thick. Lay on top, press to seal, and trim the edges.

15 Poke a hole in the top. Roll a piece of foil into a tube and place in the hole. The foil creates a chimney, allowing steam to escape from the pie while it is baking.

16 Cut out strips 1in (2.5cm) wide from the dough trimmings and cut them into leaf shapes. Mark the veins with a knife.

17 Arrange the leaves in a circle, glaze, and bake for one hour. Reduce the oven temperature to 350°F (180°C) and bake for another 30 minutes.

18 Discard the foil chimney and leave to cool before taking the pie out of the pan. Serve at room temperature.

Cornish pasties

Invented in Cornwall, England, by mine workers, the traditional crusty handle (rippled top) kept miners from getting their food grubby. Now we can eat the whole pasty!

Level rating

How long?   20 mins prep,
                1 hr chilling,
                45 mins baking

How many?   4

TRY THIS

For a veggie option, use grated Cheddar cheese instead of skirt steak. Omit the Worcestershire sauce and use vegetable shortening instead of lard.

Top tip

These will keep in the fridge for up to two days.

Ingredients

7 tbsp lard, chilled and diced

4 tbsp unsalted butter, chilled and diced

2¼ cups all-purpose flour, plus extra for dusting

½ tsp salt

1 large egg, beaten, for glazing

For the filling

9oz (250g) skirt steak, trimmed, cut into ½in (1cm) cubes

2¾oz (80g) rutabaga, peeled, and cut into ¼in (5mm) cubes

3½oz (100g) waxy potatoes, peeled, and cut into ¼in (5mm) cubes

1 large onion, finely chopped

splash of Worcestershire sauce

1 tsp all-purpose flour

sea salt and freshly ground black pepper

1 Rub the lard and butter into the flour in a bowl until it forms fine crumbs. Add the salt and enough cold water to bring the mixture together to make a soft dough.

2 Knead the dough briefly on a lightly floured surface. Wrap in plastic wrap and chill for one hour. Preheat the oven to 375°F (190°C).

3 Mix all the filling ingredients together in a bowl and season well.

4 On a floured work surface, roll the dough out to a thickness of ¼in (5mm). Using a small plate, cut four circles.

5 Fold the circles in half, then open them out again, leaving a slight fold down the center.

6 Pile one-quarter of the filling into each circle, leaving a ¾in (2cm) border all around. Brush the border of the pastry with the egg.

7 Pull both edges up over the filling and press together to seal. Crimp the sealed edge with your fingers. Brush the egg over the pasties. Bake for 40–45 minutes on a baking sheet, until golden. Cool for 15 minutes before eating.

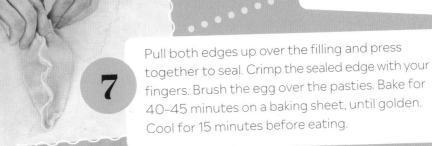

CREATIVE COOKIES AND TASTY TREATS

Bake scrumptious bars, cookies, and shortbreads. Then exercise your meringue-whipping muscles to make perfect pavlovas and marvelous macarons.

Crafty cookies

By adding a few different ingredients to this basic cookie dough, you can have a variety of tasty treats. Turn to pages 180–181 to see the extras you can add.

Turn to pages 180–181 to see the extras you can add.

Level rating

How long? 10 mins prep, 15 mins baking

How many? 16

Ingredients

7 tbsp butter, softened

½ cup granulated sugar

1 large egg

½ tsp vanilla extract

1¼ cups self-rising flour

see pages 180–181 for the extra ingredients to add to the cookie dough

1

Preheat the oven to 350°F (180°C).

2 Line two baking sheets with parchment paper.

3 Cream the butter and sugar together in a bowl with an electric mixer, then beat in the egg and vanilla extract.

4 Using a metal spoon, stir in the flour and any extra ingredients (see pages 180–181) and mix together.

5 Roll the dough into 16 balls and place on the baking sheets, leaving a little space around them. Flatten slightly and bake for 12–15 minutes.

Four ways
with cookies

Try out these tasty combinations or come up with your own cookie flavors. Make a batch and wrap them up as a present.

Level rating

How long?
10 mins prep,
15 mins baking

How many?
16

Chocolate chunks

Ingredients

Extras to add to dough recipe
2½oz (75g) dark chocolate chunks or chocolate chips
2½oz (75g) white chocolate chunks or chocolate chips

Follow the steps on page 179 and add these ingredients at Step 4.

Cinnamon and raisin

Ingredients

Extras to add to dough recipe
1 tsp ground cinnamon
4½oz (125g) raisins

Follow the steps on page 179, and add these ingredients at Step 4.

Lemon and blueberry

Ingredients

Extras to add to dough recipe

2 tsp grated lemon zest

3½oz (100g) blueberries

Follow the steps on page 179 and add these ingredients at Step 4.

White chocolate and cranberry

Ingredients

Extras to add to dough recipe

3½oz (100g) white chocolate chunks or chocolate chips

2½oz (75g) dried cranberries

Which **cookie** will **you** choose?

Follow the steps on page 179 and add these ingredients at Step 4.

Cheesy nutty biscuits

These crunchy savory biscuits are delicious served warm or cold. Serve them for lunch or as a snack, with your favorite cheese and some salad.

Level rating

How long? 10 mins prep,
1 hr chilling,
20 mins baking

How many? 24

Ingredients

4¼oz (120g) Stilton cheese, or other
   blue cheese
4 tbsp unsalted butter, softened
¾ cup all-purpose flour, sifted, plus
   extra for dusting
2oz (60g) walnuts, chopped
freshly ground black pepper
1 large egg yolk

Special equipment

2in (5cm) round cookie cutter

Top tip

The biscuits will keep in an airtight container for up to five days.

182

1 Mix the cheese and butter together in a bowl with an electric mixer until soft and creamy.

2 Add the flour to the cheese mixture and rub it in with your fingertips to form crumbs.

3 Stir in the walnuts and a grinding of black pepper. Add the egg yolk and bring the mixture together to form a stiff dough.

4 Knead the dough briefly on a lightly floured work surface. Wrap it in plastic wrap and chill for one hour. Preheat the oven to 350°F (180°C).

5 Turn the dough onto a floured work surface and knead it briefly to soften slightly. Roll it out to a thickness of ¼in (5mm) and cut out the biscuits with the cookie cutter.

6 Put the rounds on nonstick baking sheets and bake for 15 minutes. Turn them over and bake for another five minutes, until golden brown. Let them cool a little on their sheets, then move to a wire rack to cool completely, or serve warm.

Hazelnut and raisin oat cookies

These crunchy and chewy cookies are a somewhat healthier alternative to chocolate chip cookies. They're perfect to take along on a picnic.

Ingredients

3½oz (100g) hazelnuts

7 tbsp unsalted butter, softened

1 cup light brown sugar

1 large egg, beaten

1 tsp vanilla extract

1 tbsp honey

¾ cup self-rising flour, sifted

4½oz (125g) jumbo rolled oats

pinch of salt

3½oz (100g) raisins

a little milk, if needed

1 Preheat the oven to 375°F (190°C). Roast the hazelnuts in the oven on a baking sheet for five minutes.

2 Once roasted, rub with a clean dish towel to remove most of the skins.

3 Coarsely chop the hazelnuts and then set aside.

4 Cream together the butter and sugar with an electric mixer until smooth.

5 Add the egg, vanilla extract, and honey, and beat again until smooth.

6 Combine the flour, oats, and salt in a separate bowl, and stir to mix.

7 Stir the flour mix into the creamed mixture and beat until well combined.

8 Add the chopped nuts and raisins, and mix until evenly distributed.

9 If the mixture is too stiff, add a little milk until it is easier to work with.

10 Line two or three baking sheets with parchment paper. Roll the dough into 18 small balls.

11 Place the balls on the baking sheets and flatten them slightly, leaving plenty of space between them.

12 Bake for 10–15 minutes, until golden. Move to a wire rack to cool.

Top tip

The cookies will keep in an airtight container for up to five days.

Butter cookies

These deliciously buttery cookies are quick and simple to make, leaving you plenty of time for the fun part—eating them!

Level rating

How long?   15 mins prep,
                 15 mins baking

How many?   30

Ingredients

½ cup granulated sugar

1½ cups all-purpose flour, sifted, plus extra for dusting

11 tbsp unsalted butter, softened and diced

1 large egg yolk

1 tsp vanilla extract

Special equipment

2¾in (7cm) round cookie cutter

Top tip

The cookies will keep in an airtight container for up to five days.

1

Preheat the oven to 350°F (180°C).

2

Put the sugar, flour, and butter into a large bowl and rub them together until the mixture looks like fine bread crumbs.

3

Add the egg yolk and vanilla extract, and bring the mixture together into a dough. Put the dough onto a lightly floured work surface and knead it briefly, until smooth.

4

Flour the dough and work surface well, and roll the dough out to a thickness of about ¼in (5mm). If it is too sticky, chill it for 15 minutes, then try again.

5

Use the cookie cutter to cut out the cookies and place them on two or three nonstick baking sheets. Reroll the excess dough and cut out cookies until all the dough is used.

6

Bake for 10–15 minutes, until golden brown. Leave the cookies to cool until just firm, then move to a wire rack to cool completely.

Shortbread triangles

A Scottish classic, this shortbread is deliciously sweet and buttery—perfect for sharing with your friends and family.

Ingredients

11 tbsp unsalted butter, softened,
   plus extra for greasing
¼ cup granulated sugar,
   plus extra for sprinkling
1 cup all-purpose flour
½ cup cornstarch

Special equipment

8in (20cm) loose-bottomed round cake pan

1 Grease the pan and line the bottom and sides with parchment paper.

2 Put the softened butter and sugar in a large bowl.

3 Cream together the butter and sugar with an electric mixer until light and fluffy.

4 Stir in the flour and cornstarch very gently, stopping as soon as the flours are mixed in.

5 Bring the mixture together with your hands to form a very rough, crumbly dough. Put in the pan.

6 Firmly push the dough down with your hands to form a compact, even layer.

7 With a sharp knife, carefully score the circle of shortbread into eight triangles.

9 Cover the shortbread with plastic wrap and chill for one hour. Preheat the oven to 325°F (160°C).

8 Prick the shortbread all over with a fork to make a decorative pattern.

10 Bake for 30–40 minutes. Cover with foil if it browns quickly.

11 Take the shortbread out of the oven and carefully score the triangles again with a sharp knife.

12 While still warm, sprinkle a thin layer of granulated sugar evenly over the top. When cooled, turn out of the pan and cut into triangles along the scored lines.

Gingerbread cookies

This recipe is quick to make and the dough is really easy to handle. Use different cookie cutters if you want to make other shapes.

Level rating 🧁🧁

How long?   20 mins prep, 12 mins baking

How many?   16

Ingredients

¼ cup golden syrup

1⅔ cups all-purpose flour, plus extra for dusting

1 tsp baking soda

1½ tsp ground ginger

1½ tsp pumpkin pie spice

7 tbsp unsalted butter, softened and diced

¾ cup dark brown sugar

1 large egg

raisins, to decorate

⅔ cup confectioners' sugar, sifted (optional)

Special equipment

4½in (11cm) gingerbreadman cutter

piping bag with thin nozzle (optional)

1 Preheat the oven to 375°F (190°C). Heat the golden syrup until it melts, then cool.

2 Sift the flour, baking soda, and spices into a bowl. Add the butter and rub together with your fingertips to form fine crumbs.

3 Add the sugar to the flour mixture and mix well.

4 Beat the egg into the cooled syrup until well blended.

5 Make a well in the flour mixture. Pour in the syrup mix. Bring together to form a rough dough.

6 On a lightly floured work surface, knead the dough briefly, until smooth.

7 Flour the dough and the work surface well, and roll the dough out to a thickness of ¼in (5mm). Using the cutter, cut out as many shapes as possible. Put on nonstick baking sheets.

8 Decorate the cookies with raisins, giving them eyes, a nose, and buttons down the front.

9 Bake for 10–12 minutes, until golden. Put on a wire rack to cool completely.

10 If using, mix the confectioners' sugar in a bowl with enough water to form the icing. Put the icing in the piping bag.

Top tip

These gingerbread cookies will keep in an airtight container for up to three days.

11 Decorate the cookies with the piped icing to resemble clothes, hair, or whatever you like.

12 Let the icing set completely before serving or storing.

Gingerbread house

This beautiful gingerbread house is the perfect wintry centerpiece. Trace the templates from the end of this book to get the shapes just right.

Level rating

How long?   30 mins prep,
                    13 mins baking,
                    1 day assembling

How many?   8

Ingredients

⅔ cup golden syrup

8 tbsp unsalted butter, plus extra for greasing

¾ cup dark brown sugar

3¼ cups all-purpose flour, sifted, plus extra for dusting

1 tsp ground cinnamon

4 tsp ground ginger

4 tsp baking soda, dissolved in 4 tsp cold water

2 large egg yolks

For the icing

3 large egg whites

1 tsp lemon juice, plus extra if needed

7 cups confectioners' sugar, sifted

red coloring paste (optional)

Special equipment

traced templates from the end of this book (photocopy the templates, enlarging them by 200 percent, and cut them out)

tree-shaped cookie cutters

1 Melt the syrup, butter, and sugar in a saucepan. In a large bowl, sift together the flour, cinnamon, and ginger. Make a well in the center.

2 Stir in the soda mix, yolks, and melted syrup mix. Knead into a dough on a floured surface. Preheat the oven to 350°F (180°C). Lightly grease and line a baking sheet.

3 Roll out the dough to a thickness of ¼in (5mm). Put the templates on the dough and carefully cut around them using a sharp knife.

Festive treat

4 Roll out the dough trimmings and cut out tree shapes. Put all the pieces on the baking sheet. Bake for 10–13 minutes, until firm and just beginning to brown at the edges. Trim any rough edges with a sharp, hot knife.

5 Using an electric mixer, beat the egg whites in a large bowl. Stir in the lemon juice. Gradually add the confectioners' sugar.

6 Beat until the icing is smooth and pastelike. Add extra juice if it's too thick. Put one tablespoon aside and color it red.

7 Once the gingerbread pieces are cool, pipe on your designs before you assemble.

8 To assemble, work on the board that the gingerbread house will be presented on. Start from the bottom and work upward, applying icing to the seams with a palette knife.

9 Allow each seam to dry. Make sure the bottom is dry before you attach the roof. Hold the roof in place for a few minutes. Once dry, pipe it with the icing to create snow and icicles.

Be inventive with YOUR DESIGN.

Set the scene with THE EXTRA COOKIES.

193

French shortbread

These all-butter French treats are called *sablés*, or "sandy," because of their delicious crumbly texture. Use them to sandwich ice cream, as shown here, dip them in chocolate, or enjoy them on their own.

Top tip

You can prepare and store the dough, wrapped and in the fridge, up to three days ahead. Or freeze it for up to three months.

Ingredients

1¾ cups all-purpose flour, plus extra
   for dusting
½ cup granulated sugar
11 tbsp unsalted butter,
   softened and diced
1 large egg yolk
1 tsp vanilla extract
vanilla ice cream, to serve
blueberries, to serve

Special equipment

2¾in (7cm) round pastry cutter

194

1

Preheat the oven to 350°F (180°C).

2

Sift the flour into a large bowl and mix in the sugar. Rub in the butter until it looks like bread crumbs. Add the egg yolk and vanilla extract. Form into a soft dough.

3

On a lightly floured surface, briefly knead the dough until smooth. Roll it out to a thickness of ¼in (5mm).

If the **DOUGH** is too **STICKY** to roll, **CHILL** it for **15 MINUTES** and try again.

4

Use the pastry cutter to cut out 30 circles and transfer them to nonstick baking sheets.

REROLL the **SCRAPS** to the same thickness and **CUT OUT** more **CIRCLES**.

5

Bake in batches for 10–15 minutes, until the shortbread is golden brown at the edges. Cool briefly on the baking sheets. Move to a wire rack to cool completely. Sandwich the sablés with ice cream and serve with blueberries.

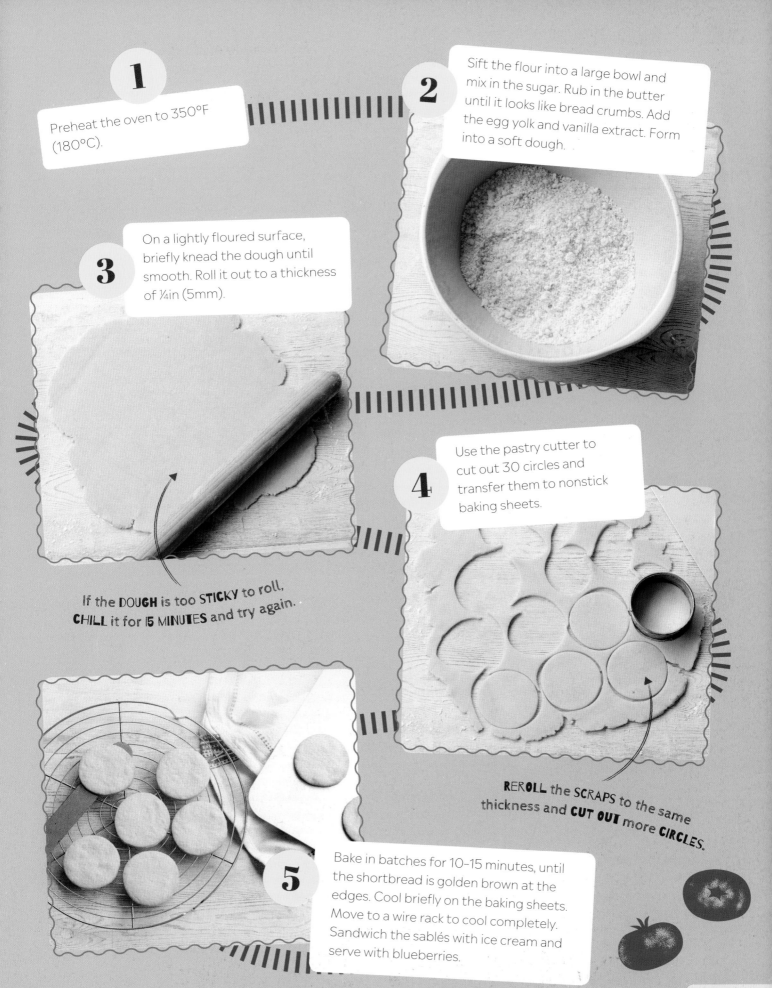

Oat bars

These chewy bars are great energy boosters and very simple to make, using only a few ingredients from your cupboard.

Level rating

How long?   15 mins prep,
                40 mins baking

How many?   16-20

Ingredients

16 tbsp butter, plus extra for greasing

1¼ cups light brown sugar

2 tbsp golden syrup

3¾ cups rolled oats

Special equipment

10in (25cm) square cake pan

1 Preheat the oven to 300°F (150°C). Lightly grease the bottom and sides of the pan.

2 Put the butter, sugar, and syrup in a large saucepan over medium heat.

3 Stir constantly with a wooden spoon to prevent scorching. Remove from the heat.

4 Stir in the oats, making sure they are well coated, but do not overwork the mix.

5 Spoon the oat mixture from the saucepan into the prepared pan.

6 Press down firmly with the wooden spoon to make a roughly even layer.

7 To neaten the surface, dip a tablespoon in hot water and use the back to smooth the top.

8 Bake for 40 minutes, or until evenly golden; you may need to turn the pan in the oven.

9 Leave to cool for 10 minutes. Cut into 16-20 squares and leave to cool in the pan. Take them out with a metal spatula.

Top tip

These will keep in an airtight container for up to one week.

Granola bars

These chunky treats are great for breakfast or as a quick snack. The peanut butter and dates make them really soft and chewy!

Level rating

How long?   15 mins prep,
                24 mins baking

How many?   16

Ingredients

vegetable oil, for greasing
3 cups rolled oats
3½oz (100g) almonds, roughly chopped
2½oz (75g) mixed seeds, such as sunflower,
    pumpkin, and sesame
½ cup honey
½ cup crunchy peanut butter
3½oz (100g) pitted dates
3½oz (100g) dried mixed berries, such
    as blueberries, cherries, cranberries,
    and raisins

Special equipment

11 x 7in (28 x 18cm) baking pan
food processor

Store any leftover BARS in an AIRTIGHT container.

1 Preheat the oven to 350°F (180°C).

2 Lightly oil the baking pan and add the oats, almonds, and seeds. Bake for 10–12 minutes.

3 Warm the honey and peanut butter in a pan over low heat. Stir occasionally until combined.

4 Put the dates, ¼ cup of warm water, and the honey mixture in a food processor and blend until smooth.

Allow to **COOL** slightly, then **CUT INTO BARS** and leave to **SET** in the pan.

5 Mix the date and oat mixtures in a bowl with the berries and stir until combined. Spoon into a pan and flatten with the back of a spoon. Bake for 12 minutes.

Chocolate fudge brownies

The best kind of brownie is crisp on the surface and soft on the inside. If you like them really gooey, bake them for five minutes less. If you like them firm, add five minutes to the baking time.

Ingredients

8 tbsp unsalted butter, plus extra
   for greasing
6oz (175g) dark chocolate,
   finely chopped
2oz (60g) very dark chocolate,
   at least 85 percent cocoa,
   finely chopped
2 tsp vanilla extract
¾ cup granulated sugar
⅓ cup dark brown sugar
2 large eggs
1 cup all-purpose flour
3 tbsp cocoa powder
¾ tsp salt
¼ tsp baking powder
2oz (60g) milk chocolate chips
2oz (60g) white chocolate chips
vanilla ice cream, to serve (optional)

Special equipment

8in (20cm) square cake pan

1

Preheat the oven to 350°F (180°C). Lightly grease the pan and line the bottom and sides with baking parchment, leaving some overhang.

2

Melt the butter and both types of chocolate in a heatproof bowl over a saucepan of simmering water, making sure it does not touch the water. Stir until smooth, then leave to cool.

3

Add the vanilla extract and both types of sugar to the mixture and whisk well. Beat in the eggs, one at a time, until smooth. Put the flour, cocoa powder, salt, and baking powder in a separate bowl and mix well.

4

Fold the dry ingredients into the chocolate mixture and combine until smooth. Mix in both types of chocolate chips until evenly mixed. Pour the mixture into the pan and spread it out evenly.

5

Bake for 40–45 minutes, until a skewer comes out clean. Leave to cool slightly, cut into nine squares, and remove from the pan.

Three ways
with brownies

There are lots of ways to make a simple brownie recipe even better and superrich. These delicious brownies are sure to be eaten in no time!

Level rating

How long?
15 mins prep,
45 mins baking (Cheesecake),
35 mins baking (Raspberry and Blondies)

How many?
9 (Cheesecake)
24 (Raspberry and Blondies)

Cheesecake brownies

Ingredients

6 tbsp unsalted butter
2½oz (75g) dark chocolate, finely chopped
1½oz (45g) very dark chocolate (90 percent cocoa), finely chopped
⅔ cup granulated sugar
2 tbsp dark brown sugar
2 large eggs
1½ tsp vanilla extract
⅔ cup all-purpose flour
½ tsp salt
½ tsp baking powder

For the cheesecake swirl

8oz (225g) full-fat cream cheese
1 tsp vanilla extract
pinch of salt
1 large egg yolk
⅓ cup confectioners' sugar

Special equipment

8in (20cm) square cake pan, greased and lined with parchment paper, leaving some overhang

1 Preheat the oven to 350°F (180°C).

2 Melt the butter and both types of chocolate in a heatproof bowl over a saucepan of simmering water.

3 Leave it to cool, then slowly beat in both types of sugar to combine. Beat in the eggs and vanilla extract. Fold in the flour, salt, and baking powder.

4 Beat the cheesecake swirl ingredients in a separate bowl. Pour the chocolate mixture in the pan. Spoon the cheesecake mixture on top and swirl the tip of a knife through it.

5 Bake for 40–45 minutes. Cool, take out of the pan, and cut into nine portions. Serve warm.

CHEESECAKE swirls are SUPERRICH!

202

Chocolate and raspberry brownies

Ingredients

8 tbsp unsalted butter
8oz (225g) dark chocolate, finely chopped
1 cup dark brown sugar
½ cup granulated sugar
2 tsp vanilla extract
4 large eggs
1 cup all-purpose flour
1 tsp salt
1 tsp baking powder
8oz (225g) raspberries
5oz (140g) milk chocolate chips

Special equipment
12in (30cm) baking pan, greased and lined
   with parchment paper, leaving some overhang

1 Preheat the oven to 350°F (180°C).

2 Melt the butter and chocolate in a heatproof bowl over a saucepan of simmering water. Cool slightly, then mix in the two types of sugar and the vanilla.

3 Beat in the eggs, one at a time. Fold in the flour, salt, and baking powder. Gently stir in the raspberries and chocolate chips. Mix well and pour into the pan in an even layer.

4 Bake for 30–35 minutes. Let the brownies cool slightly in the pan, then take out. Cut into 24 pieces. Serve warm.

RASPBERRIES make it extra GOOEY!

Pecan blondies

Ingredients

10 tbsp unsalted butter
1½ cups light brown sugar
1½ tsp vanilla extract
3 large eggs
1⅔ cups all-purpose flour
1 tsp salt
1¼ tsp baking powder
4½oz (125g) chopped pecans
6oz (175g) white chocolate chips

Special equipment
12in (30cm) baking pan, greased and lined
   with parchment paper, leaving some overhang

1 Preheat the oven to 350°F (180°C).

2 Melt the butter in a saucepan over low heat. Take off the heat and add the sugar and vanilla. Beat until combined. Add the eggs, one at a time, beating well after each addition, until the mixture is smooth.

3 In another bowl, combine the flour, salt, and baking powder. Pour in the butter mixture and fold in until combined. Add the pecans and chocolate chips, mixing evenly. Pour the mixture into the pan.

4 Bake for 30 minutes, until a skewer comes out clean. Let the brownies cool slightly in the pan, then take out. Cut into 24 pieces. Serve warm.

Strawberries and cream macarons

The art of macaron making can seem tricky, but this recipe is super simple to make and creates picture-perfect results.

Top tip

Unfilled macaron shells can be stored for up to three days.

Level rating 🧁🧁

How long? 30 mins prep, 20 mins baking

How many? 20

Ingredients

¾ cup ground almonds
½ cup confectioners' sugar
2 large egg whites, at room temperature
⅓ cup granulated sugar

For the filling

1 cup heavy cream
5–10 very large strawberries, preferably the same width as the macarons

Special equipment

food processor with blade attachment
piping bag with small, plain nozzle

1 Preheat the oven to 300°F (150°C). Line two baking sheets with parchment paper.

2 Trace 20 x 1¼in (3cm) circles on both sheets of parchment paper, leaving 1¼in (3cm) between the circles. Turn the parchment paper over.

3 In a food processor, pulse together the almonds and confectioners' sugar to a very fine powder.

4 In a large, clean bowl, beat the egg whites to stiff peaks using an electric mixer.

5 Add the granulated sugar a little at a time, beating well between additions.

6 The meringue mixture should be very stiff at this point.

7 Gently fold in the almond mixture a spoonful at a time, until just mixed in.

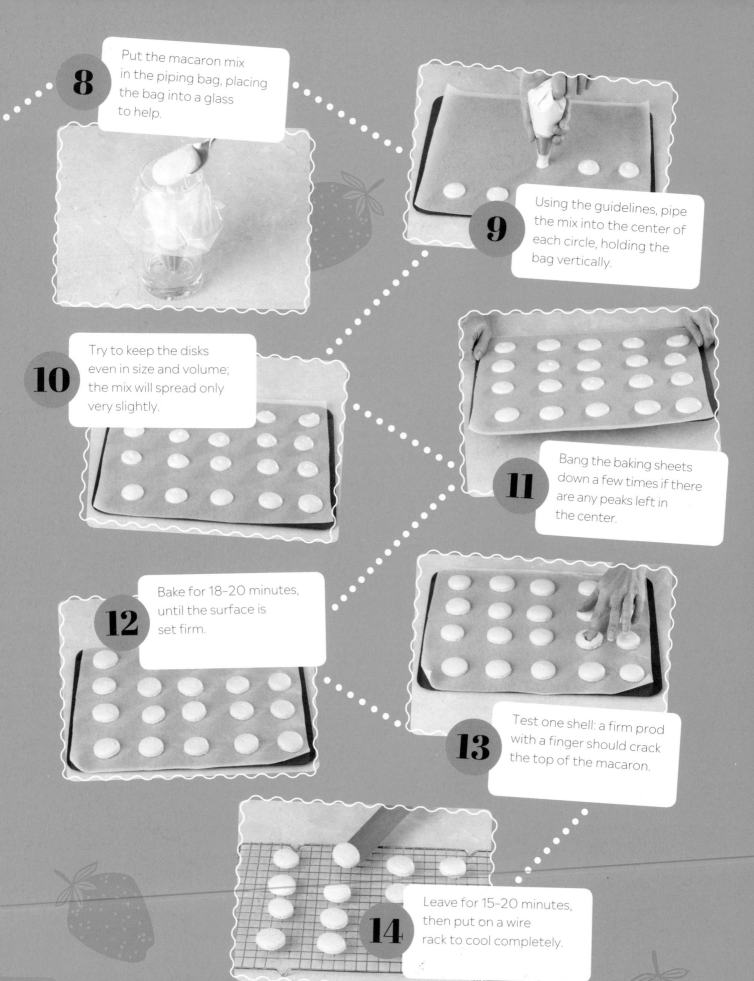

8 Put the macaron mix in the piping bag, placing the bag into a glass to help.

9 Using the guidelines, pipe the mix into the center of each circle, holding the bag vertically.

10 Try to keep the disks even in size and volume; the mix will spread only very slightly.

11 Bang the baking sheets down a few times if there are any peaks left in the center.

12 Bake for 18–20 minutes, until the surface is set firm.

13 Test one shell: a firm prod with a finger should crack the top of the macaron.

14 Leave for 15–20 minutes, then put on a wire rack to cool completely.

15 Beat the cream until thick; a soft whip will ooze out the sides and soften the shells.

16 Transfer the cream into the (cleaned) piping bag used earlier, with the same nozzle.

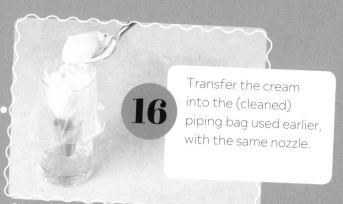

17 Pipe a dollop of the whipped cream onto the flat side of half the macarons.

18 Slice the strawberries widthwise into thin slices, the same size as the macarons.

19 Put a slice of strawberry on top of the cream filling of each macaron.

20 Add the remaining macaron shells and sandwich gently. The fillings should peek out.

Serve right away.

Three ways
with macarons

With the skills you've learned on pages 204–207, become a macaron master and try out these tasty new flavors to serve at a party.

Level rating

How long?
30 mins prep,
25 mins baking,
15 mins chilling (Chocolate and Pistachio)

How many?
20

Raspberry macarons

Ingredients

½ cup ground almonds
⅔ cup confectioners' sugar
2 large egg whites, at
    room temperature
⅓ cup granulated sugar
¼ tsp red food coloring paste

For the filling
5½oz (150g) mascarpone
2 tbsp heavy cream
2 tbsp confectioners' sugar
30 raspberries, halved lengthwise

The CREAM should OOZE out a bit.

TRY THIS

For a twist, use fruit other than raspberries. Match the food coloring with the fruit.

1 Follow Steps 1–14 on pages 205–206 to make the macarons. Add the red food coloring in Step 7.

2 To make the filling, beat the mascarpone, heavy cream, and confectioners' sugar in a bowl and put it into a piping bag.

3 Pipe a little of the cream filling onto 20 shells and top each with three raspberry slices.

4 Pipe the filling onto the remaining 20 shells and place on top of the raspberries to sandwich together.

Pistachio macarons

Ingredients

1¼oz (40g) unsalted and skinned
    whole pistachios

¼ cup ground almonds

⅔ cup confectioners' sugar

2 large egg whites, at room temperature

⅓ cup granulated sugar

¼ tsp green food coloring paste

For the ganache filling

4½oz (125g) white chocolate, finely chopped

3 tbsp heavy cream

1 tsp unsalted butter

Top tip

To remove the skin from the pistachios, rub the nuts with a clean dish towel before grinding them.

1 Follow Steps 1–14 on pages 205–206. Before Step 3, pulse the pistachios in a food processor to a coarse powder. Then add the ground almonds and confectioners' sugar and pulse to a fine powder. Add the green food coloring in Step 7.

2 For the filling, melt the chocolate, cream, and butter in a heatproof bowl over a saucepan of simmering water. Beat with a wooden spoon until thick and shiny. Put into a piping bag and chill for 15 minutes.

3 Pipe a little of the chocolate ganache onto 20 shells and then sandwich together with the remaining 20 shells.

Chocolate macarons

Ingredients

½ cup ground almonds

¼ cup cocoa powder

⅔ cup confectioners' sugar

2 large egg whites, at room temperature

⅓ cup granulated sugar

For the ganache filling

⅓ cup heavy cream

3½oz (100g) bittersweet chocolate,
    finely chopped

1 Follow Steps 1–14 on pages 205–206. Add the cocoa powder in Step 7.

2 For the filling, heat the cream in a heavy-bottomed saucepan until hot, but not boiling.

3 Take off the heat and mix in the chocolate so it melts completely. Put into a piping bag and chill for 15 minutes.

4 Pipe a little of the chocolate ganache onto 20 shells and then sandwich with the remaining shells.

Raspberry cream meringues

These mini meringues are filled with fresh raspberries and whipped cream—they are great for a summery treat.

Ingredients

4 large egg whites, at room temperature
1 cup + 1 tbsp granulated sugar, or double
   the weight of the egg whites

For the filling

3½oz (100g) raspberries
1¼ cups heavy cream
1 tbsp confectioners' sugar, sifted

Special equipment

metal mixing bowl
piping bag with plain nozzle

1 Preheat the oven to 250°F (120°C). Line a baking sheet with parchment paper.

2 Weigh the egg whites. You will need exactly double the weight of sugar to egg whites.

3 Beat the egg whites in the metal bowl with an electric mixer until they are stiff and form strong peaks.

4 Add half the sugar, a couple of tablespoons at a time, beating in between each addition.

5 Gently fold the rest of the sugar into the egg whites, trying to keep the air in. Put the mixture into a piping bag with a plain nozzle.

6 Pipe the mixture onto the parchment paper with a plain nozzle, leaving 2in (5cm) gaps between. Bake for one hour.

7 They are ready when they lift easily from the parchment paper and sound hollow when tapped. Put on a wire rack to cool.

8 Put the raspberries in a bowl and crush them with the back of a fork, so they break up.

9 In a separate bowl, beat the heavy cream until firm but not stiff.

10 Gently fold together the cream and crushed raspberries and combine with the confectioners' sugar.

11 Spread a little of the raspberry mixture onto half the meringues.

12 Top with the remaining meringue halves and gently press together to form sandwiches. Serve immediately.

Strawberry pavlova

This beloved dessert is surprisingly easy to make. Top with fresh strawberries and cream, or turn the page to try out different combinations.

Level rating

How long?   15 mins prep,
                1 hr 35 mins baking

How many?   8

Ingredients

6 egg whites, at room temperature
pinch of salt
1½ cups granulated sugar,
   or double the weight of the egg whites
2 tsp cornstarch
1 tsp vinegar

For the filling

1¼ cups heavy cream
strawberries, to decorate

1 Preheat the oven to 350°F (180°C). Line a baking sheet with parchment paper.

2 Draw an 8in (20cm) diameter circle on the parchment paper using a pencil. Flip the paper over, so the pencil mark doesn't transfer to the meringue.

3 Put the egg whites in a large, clean, grease-free bowl with the salt. Using an electric mixer, beat the egg whites until stiff peaks form.

4 Add the sugar, one tablespoon at a time, and beat well after each addition. Continue beating until the egg whites are stiff and glossy. Mix in the cornstarch and vinegar.

5 Spoon the mixture into a mound inside the circle on the parchment paper and spread it to the edges of the circle. Form swirls, using a palette knife, as you spread out the meringue.

6 Bake for five minutes, then reduce the oven temperature to 250°F (120°C) and bake for one and a half hours.

7 Turn the oven off and let the meringue cool completely in the oven. Whip the cream until it holds its shape.

CRISP AND CHEWY

8 Spoon the cream onto the meringue bottom and decorate with the strawberries.

Two ways
with pavlova

A fantastic way to feed a crowd, the pavlova bases here can be prepared in advance and filled at the last moment with the best of the season's fruit, or try out your own favorite fruit combinations.

Level rating

How long?
15 mins prep,
1 hr 35 mins baking

How many?
8

Chocolate, apple, and pear

Ingredients

6 egg whites, at room temperature
pinch of salt
1½ cups granulated sugar, or double the
 weight of the egg whites
2 tsp cornstarch
1 tsp vinegar
2 tbsp cocoa powder, plus extra
 for dusting

For the filling
¼ tsp ground cinnamon
1½ tsp confectioners' sugar
¼ tsp ground cardamom
3oz (85g) green apple, thinly sliced
3oz (85g) pear, thinly sliced
1 cup heavy cream

1 For the pavlova, follow Steps 1–7 on pages 212–213. Add the cocoa powder in Step 4.

2 For the filling, combine the cinnamon, confectioners' sugar, and cardamom in a bowl. Add the fruit, toss to coat, and leave for 5–10 minutes.

3 Spread the whipped cream on the pavlova. Arrange the fruit on top, sprinkle with cocoa powder, and serve immediately.

Tropical fruit

Ingredients

6 egg whites, at room temperature

pinch of salt

1½ cups granulated sugar, or double the
weight of the egg whites

2 tsp cornstarch

1 tsp vinegar

For the filling

1¼ cups heavy cream

14oz (400g) mango and papaya, peeled
and chopped

2 passion fruits

1 For the pavlova,
follow Steps 1–7 on
pages 212–213.

2 For the filling, whip the cream until
it holds its shape. Top the pavlova
with the cream, then add the
chopped tropical fruits.

3 Halve the passion fruits and
squeeze out the juice and
seeds over the pavlova just
before serving.

Lemon meringue pie

This family favorite has crunchy pie crust layered with a tangy lemon filling and a soft meringue topping. It's a taste sensation!

1 Mix the flour, sugar, salt, and butter together in a large bowl. Pour in the vinegar mix. Use two forks to fluff it, until clumps form. Knead the dough briefly and wrap it in plastic wrap. Chill for 30 minutes.

2 On a floured surface, roll the pie dough into a circle ⅛in (3mm) thick. Grease and line the pan with the crust. Prick the crust. Chill for 30 minutes. Preheat the oven to 375°F (190°C). Line the pie crust with parchment paper and fill with baking beans. Bake for 25 minutes.

3 Remove the beans and parchment paper. Bake for 6–10 minutes, until golden. Let cool. Reduce the oven temperature to 350°F (180°C).

4 For the filling, put the flour, sugar, salt, and cornstarch in a pan. Slowly whisk in 1¼ cups water until smooth. Cook for 5–6 minutes over medium heat, bring to a boil, then reduce the heat. Cook for one minute. Whisk a little mixture into the yolks.

Level rating

How long? 30 mins prep,
1 hr chilling,
50 mins baking

How many? 8

Ingredients

1¼ cups all-purpose flour, plus extra
  for dusting
1 tbsp granulated sugar
½ tsp salt
8 tbsp unsalted butter, chilled
  and grated, plus extra for greasing
1 tsp apple cider vinegar, whisked with
  ¼ cup chilled water

For the filling

3 tbsp all-purpose flour
¾ cup granulated sugar
¼ tsp salt
¼ cup cornstarch
5 large egg yolks, beaten
1 tbsp unsalted butter
grated zest of 2 lemons
½ cup lemon juice

For the meringue

4 large egg whites
⅛ tsp salt
¼ tsp cream of tartar
½ cup granulated sugar
1 tbsp cornstarch

Special equipment

9in (23cm) fluted pie pan, about
  2in (5cm) deep
baking beans

5 Stir a little more hot mixture into the yolk mixture, then pour the yolk mixture into the pan. Bring to a boil, stirring. Reduce the heat and cook for one minute. Remove from the heat and whisk in the butter, zest, and lemon juice. Cover and keep warm.

6 For the meringue, whisk the egg whites and salt in a bowl until foamy. Then whisk in the cream of tartar until the mixture forms soft peaks. Combine the sugar and cornstarch in a small bowl and whisk into the egg white mixture until it forms stiff, glossy peaks.

7 Pour the filling into the pie crust. Spoon the meringue onto the filling. Bake for 15 minutes, until browned. Cool on a wire rack before serving.

CLASSIC CRUSTS

Roll up your sleeves and get ready
to master a variety of loaves,
flatbreads, rolls, and baguettes.
Refer to the technique pages
at the beginning of this book
for tips on how to make the
best bread ever!

Basic white bread

This basic dough recipe can be made into a delicious traditional loaf or rolls. Replace the bread flour with whole-wheat bread flour if you want to make whole-wheat bread.

Level rating

How long?   45 mins prep,
3 hrs 15 mins rising and
proofing, 40 mins baking

How many?   2 loaves

Ingredients

For the sponge

2½ tsp dried yeast, dissolved in
¼ cup lukewarm water
¾ cup bread flour, plus extra
for dusting

For the bread

2 cups lukewarm milk, plus extra
for glazing
4 cups bread flour, plus extra
for dusting
1 tbsp salt
butter, melted, for greasing

Special equipment

2 x 2lb (900g) loaf pans

1 Put the dissolved yeast mix and 1 cup + 2 tbsp lukewarm water into a large bowl. Stir in the flour and mix well with your hands for about a minute.

2 Sprinkle two tablespoons of flour over the sponge. Cover the bowl with a damp dish towel and leave it in a warm place for 30–60 minutes, until bubbles appear on the surface.

3 Mixing with your hands, add the milk to the sponge. Mix in half the flour and the salt. Then add the remaining flour.

4 On a floured work surface, knead the dough by holding it with one hand and pushing it away from you with the other.

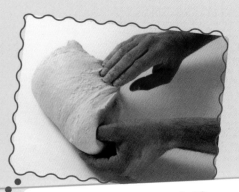

5 Continue kneading for 8-10 minutes, until the dough is smooth and elastic. If the dough sticks while kneading, flour the work surface.

7 Grease the pans with melted butter. Punch down the dough. Halve the dough and put each half into a pan. Cover the pans with a dry dish towel and leave to rise in a warm place for 45 minutes.

6 Put the dough in a large bowl. Cover with a damp dish towel and leave to rise in a warm place for 1–1½ hours, until doubled in size.

8 Preheat the oven to 425°F (220°C). Brush the loaves with milk. Using a sharp knife, carefully make a light cut along the length of each loaf. Bake for 20 minutes.

9 Reduce the oven temperature to 375°F (190°C). Bake for another 15–20 minutes, until golden brown. Tap the bottom with your knuckles; the bread should sound hollow. Put on a wire rack to cool.

TRY THIS

At Step 7 divide the dough into eight balls. Put on a baking sheet. Cover with a damp dish towel. Leave to rise for 30 minutes. Brush milk over the rolls. Bake for 25 minutes.

Whole-wheat cottage loaf

Stone-ground whole-wheat flour makes this lovely loaf more filling than simple white bread, and it has a delicious flavor!

Super soft!

Level rating

How long? 40 mins prep, 2 hrs 15 mins rising and proofing, 45 mins baking

How many? 2 loaves

Ingredients

- 4 tbsp unsalted butter, plus extra for greasing
- 3 tbsp honey
- 3 tsp dried yeast
- 1 tbsp salt
- 3¼ cups stone-ground whole-wheat bread flour
- 1 cup bread flour, plus extra for dusting

222

1 Melt the butter. Mix one tablespoon of honey and ¼ cup lukewarm water in a bowl.

2 Sprinkle the yeast over the honey mixture. Leave it for five minutes to dissolve, stirring once.

3 Mix together the butter, yeast, salt, remaining honey, and 1¾ cups lukewarm water.

4 Stir in half the whole wheat flour and all the bread flour, and mix it with your hands.

5 Add the remaining whole wheat flour, ¾ cup at a time, mixing after each addition.

6 The dough should be soft and slightly sticky and pull away from the sides of the bowl.

7 Turn the dough onto a floured work surface and sprinkle it with flour.

8 Knead for 10 minutes until it is very smooth, elastic, and makes a ball.

9 Grease a large bowl with butter. Put in the dough and flip it to butter the surface lightly.

10 Cover with a damp dish towel. Leave it in a warm place for 1–1½ hours, until doubled in size.

11 Grease two baking sheets. Place the dough on a floured work surface and punch it down.

12 Cover and let it rest for five minutes. Cut it into three equal pieces, then cut one piece in half.

13 Cover one large and one small piece of dough with a dish towel and shape the rest.

14 Shape one large piece into a loose ball. Fold in the sides, turn, and pinch to make a tight ball.

15 Put the ball, seam-side down, onto the baking sheet.

16 Similarly, shape one small piece into a ball. Set it, seam-side down, on top of the first ball.

17 Using your forefinger, press through the center of the balls down to the baking sheet.

18 Repeat with the remaining two dough balls to shape a second loaf.

19 Cover both loaves with dish towels. Leave in a warm place for 45 minutes, or until doubled in size.

20 Preheat the oven to 375°F (190°C). Bake for 40–45 minutes, until well browned.

21 The loaves should sound hollow when tapped on the bottom. Cool on a wire rack.

Rye bread

This crusty German loaf is more chewy and has a stronger flavor than bread made from wheat flour.

Level rating

How long?   40 mins prep,
                2 hrs 45 mins rising
                and proofing,
                55 mins baking

How many?   1 loaf

1 Put the dissolved yeast, molasses, two-thirds of the caraway seeds, salt, and oil into a bowl.

Ingredients

2½ tsp dried yeast, dissolved in
    ¼ cup lukewarm water
1 tbsp dark molasses
1 tbsp caraway seeds
2 tsp salt
1 tbsp vegetable oil, plus extra
    for greasing
1 cup sparkling water
1⅓ cups rye flour
1 cup bread flour, plus extra
    for dusting
polenta (fine yellow cornmeal),
    for dusting
1 egg white, beaten until frothy,
    for glazing

2 Pour in the sparkling water. Stir in the rye flour and mix together well with your hands.

3 Gradually add the bread flour until it forms a soft, slightly sticky dough.

4 Knead for 8–10 minutes on a floured surface, until smooth and elastic, and put in an oiled bowl.

6 Sprinkle a baking sheet with polenta. Punch down the dough on a floured work surface.

5 Cover with a damp dish towel. Put in a warm place for 1½–2 hours, until doubled in size.

7 Cover with plastic wrap and let it rest for five minutes. Pat the dough into an oval about 10in (25cm) long.

8 Roll it back and forth on the work surface, putting pressure on the ends to make them narrower.

9 Put on a baking sheet. Cover with plastic wrap and leave in a warm place for 45 minutes, until doubled in size.

10 Preheat the oven to 375°F (190°C). Brush the beaten egg over the loaf to glaze.

11 Sprinkle with the remaining caraway seeds and press them into the dough.

12 With a sharp knife, carefully make three diagonal slashes about ¼in (5mm) deep on top. Bake for 50–55 minutes. Put on a wire rack to cool.

Pumpkin bread

By using grated pumpkin in this quick bread, it stays moist for days! Serve it with a winter soup or summer salad.

Level rating

How long?   20 mins prep,
                  50 mins baking

How many?   1 loaf

Ingredients

2¼ cups all-purpose flour,
   plus extra for dusting

1 cup whole-wheat self-rising flour

1 tsp baking soda

½ tsp salt

4¼oz (120g) pumpkin or butternut
   squash, peeled, seeded, and
   coarsely grated

1oz (30g) pumpkin seeds

1¼ cups buttermilk

1 Preheat the oven to 425°F (220°C). In a bowl, mix both types of flour, baking soda, and salt.

2 Add the grated pumpkin and seeds. Stir well to combine, so that no lumps remain.

3 Make a well in the center and pour in the buttermilk. Stir together to form a dough.

4 Use your hands to bring the mixture together into a ball, then turn onto a floured surface.

5 Knead the dough for two minutes, until smooth. You may need to add extra flour.

6 Shape the dough into a round 6in (15cm) wide. Put on a baking sheet lined with parchment paper.

7 Use a sharp knife to carefully slash a cross into the top. This helps the bread to rise when baking.

8 Bake for 30 minutes, until risen. Reduce the temperature of the oven to 400°F (200°C).

9 Bake for another 20 minutes. When cooled, the bottom should sound hollow when you tap it.

10 Put the bread on a wire rack and allow it to cool for at least 20 minutes before serving.

Top tip

This bread will keep, well wrapped in wax paper, for up to three days. Cut the bread into wedges or slices and serve.

Ciabatta

The name "ciabatta" is the Italian word for slipper! A good ciabatta should be well risen and crusty, with large air pockets.

Level rating

How long?   30 mins prep, 3 hrs rising and proofing, 30 mins baking

How many?   2 loaves

Ingredients

2 tsp dried yeast

2 tbsp olive oil, plus extra for greasing

2½ cups bread flour, plus extra for dusting

1 tsp sea salt

1 Dissolve the yeast in 1½ cups lukewarm water, then pour in the oil.

2 Put the flour and salt in a bowl. Make a well, pour in the yeast, and stir to form a soft dough.

3 Knead on a floured surface for 10 minutes, until smooth and soft.

4 Put the dough in a lightly oiled bowl and cover loosely with plastic wrap.

5 Leave to rise in a warm place for two hours, until doubled in size. Turn onto a floured surface.

6 Gently punch down the dough, then divide it into two equal pieces.

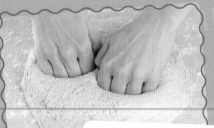

7 Knead them briefly and shape into long rectangles around 12 x 4in (30 x 10cm).

8 Place each loaf on a lined baking sheet, with enough space to allow it to expand.

9 Cover loosely with plastic wrap and a dish towel. Leave for one hour, until doubled in size.

10 Preheat the oven to 450°F (230°C). Spray the loaves with a fine mist of water.

11 Bake for 30 minutes, spraying them with water every 10 minutes.

12 The loaves are baked when the tops are golden brown and the bottoms sound hollow when tapped.

Top tip

These are best eaten the same day, but can be stored overnight, wrapped in wax paper.

Multigrain loaf

Perfect for breakfast, this tasty loaf is fun to make and nutritious. To make a white loaf, take out the whole-wheat flour and double the white bread flour.

Level rating

How long?   45 mins prep,
3 hrs rising and proofing,
45 mins baking

How many?   2 loaves

Ingredients

2½oz (75g) sunflower seeds

5 tbsp rolled oats

⅓ cup wheat bran

½ cup polenta (fine yellow cornmeal), plus extra for the baking sheets

3 tbsp light brown sugar

1 tbsp salt

2½ tsp dried yeast, dissolved in ¼ cup lukewarm water

1¾ cups lukewarm buttermilk

1½ cups whole-wheat bread flour

1½ cups bread flour, plus extra for dusting

1 tbsp melted butter, for greasing

1 large egg white, for glazing

1   Preheat the oven to 350°F (180°C). Put the seeds on a baking sheet and roast in the oven for 5–7 minutes, until browned. Let them cool, then coarsely chop.

2   Put the sunflower seeds, rolled oats, wheat bran, polenta, brown sugar, and salt in a large bowl. Add the dissolved yeast and buttermilk and mix with your hand.

3   Stir in the whole-wheat flour and half of the white bread flour and mix well with your hand. Add the remaining white bread flour; the dough should be soft and slightly sticky.

4   Knead the dough on a well floured surface for 8–10 minutes, until it is smooth and elastic. If the dough sticks while kneading, flour the work surface again.

5   Grease a large bowl with the butter. Put the dough in the bowl and flip it to butter the surface. Cover the bowl with a damp dish towel and let the dough rise in a warm place for 1½–2 hours, until doubled in size.

6   Sprinkle two baking sheets with polenta. Put the dough on a lightly floured work surface and punch it down.

7 Cut the dough in half. With floured hands, pat one piece of dough into an 8 x 2in (20 x 5cm) rectangle, leaving the corners rounded. Put it on one of the baking sheets, then repeat to shape the remaining dough.

8 Cover with a dry dish towel and leave to rise in a warm place for about one hour, until doubled in size. Preheat the oven to 375°F (190°C). Beat the egg white until just frothy. Brush the loaves with the egg white.

9 Bake for 40–45 minutes, until well browned. Tap the bottom of the loaves with your knuckles; the bread should sound hollow. Move to a wire rack to cool completely.

SUPERSOFT INSIDE

Easy bread rolls

These rolls are easy to make and fun to shape. They are great served with butter or loaded with your favorite sandwich filling.

Level rating

How long?   55 mins prep,
2 hrs rising and proofing,
18 mins baking

How many?   16

Ingredients

⅔ cup milk

4 tbsp unsalted butter, cubed,
   plus extra for greasing

2 tbsp granulated sugar

3 tsp dried yeast

2 large eggs, plus 1 yolk, for glazing

2 tsp salt

3 cups bread flour, plus extra
   for dusting

poppy seeds, for sprinkling

1 Bring the milk to a boil. Put ¼ cup into a small bowl and let it cool to lukewarm. Add the butter and sugar to the remaining milk in the pan and stir until melted. Cool to lukewarm.

2 Sprinkle the yeast over the ¼ cup of milk. Leave for five minutes to dissolve. Stir once. In a large bowl, lightly beat the eggs. Add the sweetened milk, salt, and dissolved yeast.

3 Gradually stir in the flour until the dough forms a ball. It should be soft and slightly sticky.

4 Knead the dough on a floured work surface for 5–7 minutes, until smooth and elastic. Put in a greased bowl. Cover with plastic wrap. Put in a warm place for 1–1½ hours, until doubled in size.

6 Cut in half and roll each piece into a cylinder. Cut each cylinder into eight equal pieces.

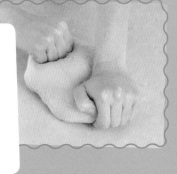

5 Line two baking sheets with parchment paper. On a floured work surface, punch down the dough.

7 To shape round rolls, roll the dough in a circular motion so it forms a smooth ball.

8 For a baker's knot, roll the dough into a rope, shape into an eight, and tuck the ends through the holes.

9 For a snail shape, roll the dough into a long rope and wind it around in a spiral, tucking the end underneath.

10 Put the rolls on the baking sheets. Cover with a dish towel. Leave in a warm place for 30 minutes.

11 Preheat the oven to 425°F (220°C). Beat the egg yolk with a tablespoon of water.

12 Brush all the rolls with the egg. Sprinkle the poppy seeds on the round rolls. Bake for 15–18 minutes, until golden brown.

SERVE WARM

Soda bread

This bread has a light, cakelike texture.
As an added bonus, it requires no kneading,
so is a wonderfully effort-free loaf.

Level rating 🧁🧁

How long? 15 mins prep,
40 mins baking

How many? 1 loaf

Ingredients

butter, for greasing
4 cups stone-ground whole-wheat flour,
  plus extra for dusting
1½ tsp baking soda
1½ tsp salt
2 cups buttermilk, plus extra
  if needed

1 Preheat the oven to 400°F (200°C). Grease a baking sheet with butter.

2 Sift the flour, baking soda, and salt into a large bowl, adding in any leftover bran.

3 Mix thoroughly to combine, then make a well in the center.

4 Slowly pour the buttermilk into the center of the well.

5 With your hands, quickly draw in the flour to make a soft, slightly sticky dough.

6 Do not overwork the dough. Add a little more buttermilk if it seems dry.

7 Turn the dough onto a floured surface and quickly shape into a round loaf.

8 Put the loaf on the baking sheet and pat it down into a round, about 2in (5cm) high.

9 Carefully make a cross ½in (1cm) deep in the top of the loaf with a sharp knife.

10 Bake the loaf for 35–40 minutes, until brown.

11 When cooked, turn the loaf over and tap the bottom. The bread should sound hollow.

12 Put the bread on a wire rack and let it cool slightly before serving.

Baguette

To create a light and soft baguette you first need to make a "sponge," which is a starter dough that rises for 12 hours. Then you add it to the other ingredients to make a delicious bread.

Level rating	
How long?	30 mins prep, 12 hrs or overnight fermenting, 3½ hrs rising and proofing, 20 mins baking
How many?	2 loaves

Ingredients

For the sponge

⅛ tsp dried yeast

½ cup white or brown bread flour

1 tbsp rye flour

vegetable oil, for greasing

For the dough

1 tsp dried yeast

2½ cups white or brown bread flour, plus extra for dusting

½ tsp salt

1 For the sponge, dissolve the yeast in ¼ cup lukewarm water and add to the two types of flour.

2 Form a sticky, loose dough and place in an oiled bowl, with room for it to expand.

3 Cover with plastic wrap and put in a cool place to rise for at least 12 hours.

4 To make the dough, dissolve the yeast in ⅔ cup lukewarm water, whisking continuously.

5 Put the risen sponge, flour, and salt into a large bowl and pour in the yeast liquid.

6 Stir it all together with a wooden spoon to form a soft dough.

7 Knead for 10 minutes on a floured surface until smooth, glossy, and elastic.

8 Put in an oiled bowl, cover with plastic wrap, and let rise in a warm place for two hours.

9 Put it on a floured surface. Punch it down. Carefully divide the dough into two equal portions.

10 Knead briefly and shape each piece into a rectangle. Tuck one short edge into the center.

11 Press down firmly, fold over the other short edge, and press firmly again.

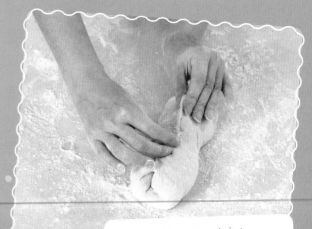

12 Shape the dough into a rounded oblong. Pinch to seal and turn seam-side down.

13 Shape into a long, thin log shape that is 1½in (4cm) wide.

14 Place the loaves on baking sheets and cover with oiled plastic wrap and a clean dish towel.

15 Keep in a warm place for 1½ hours, until doubled in size. Preheat the oven to 425°F (220°C).

16 Carefully slash each loaf deeply on the diagonal along the top.

17 Dust with a little flour, spray with water, and put the loaves in the oven.

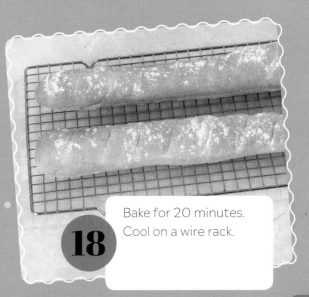

18 Bake for 20 minutes. Cool on a wire rack.

Bagels

These soft and springy bagels are perfect for breakfast or lunchtime—slice them open and spread with butter or cream cheese, or sandwich together with a filling of your choice.

Level rating

How long? 40 mins prep,
3 hrs rising and proofing,
20-25 mins baking

How many? 8-10

Ingredients

3¼ cups bread flour, plus extra for dusting

2 tsp fine salt

2 tsp granulated sugar

2 tsp dried yeast

1 tbsp sunflower oil, plus extra for greasing

1 egg, beaten, for glazing

1 Put the flour, salt, and sugar in a bowl. In a separate bowl, mix the yeast with 1¼ cups lukewarm water.

2 Add the oil to the yeast, mix and pour the liquid into the flour mixture, stirring together to form a soft dough.

3 Knead on a floured surface for 10 minutes, until smooth. Put in an oiled bowl. Cover with plastic wrap and leave in a warm place for 1-2 hours, until doubled in size.

4 Put the dough on a floured surface, press it down to its original size, and divide into 8-10 pieces.

5 Take each piece of dough and roll it under your palm to make a fat log shape.

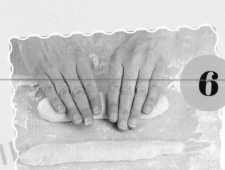

6 Using your palms, continue to roll it toward each end until it is about 10in (25cm) long.

7 Take the dough and wrap it around your knuckles, so the seam is on your palm.

8 Squeeze gently together, then roll briefly to seal up the seam. The hole should still be big at this stage. Repeat to shape all the bagels.

9 Line two baking sheets with parchment paper and put the bagels on the sheets. Cover with plastic wrap and a dish towel. Leave in a warm place for up to one hour, until doubled in size.

10 Preheat the oven to 425°F (220°C). Boil a large pan of water, then let it simmer. Cook the bagels in the water for one minute on each side.

11 Use a slotted spoon to remove the bagels from the water. Dry them briefly on a clean dish towel. Return the bagels to the baking sheets and brush them with the beaten egg.

12 Bake in the center of the oven for 20–25 minutes, until golden. Cool for at least five minutes on a wire rack before serving.

Pretzels

These traditional German breads are surprisingly easy to make. Have fun braiding the dough to create the unique pretzel shape.

Level rating	🧁🧁🧁
How long?	50 mins prep, 1½–2½ hrs rising and proofing, 20 mins baking
How many?	16

Ingredients

2¾ cups bread flour, plus extra
   for dusting
1 cup all-purpose flour
1 tsp salt
2 tbsp granulated sugar
2 tsp dried yeast
1 tbsp sunflower oil, plus extra
   for greasing

For the glaze

¼ tsp baking soda
coarse sea salt or 2 tbsp sesame seeds
1 egg, beaten, for glazing

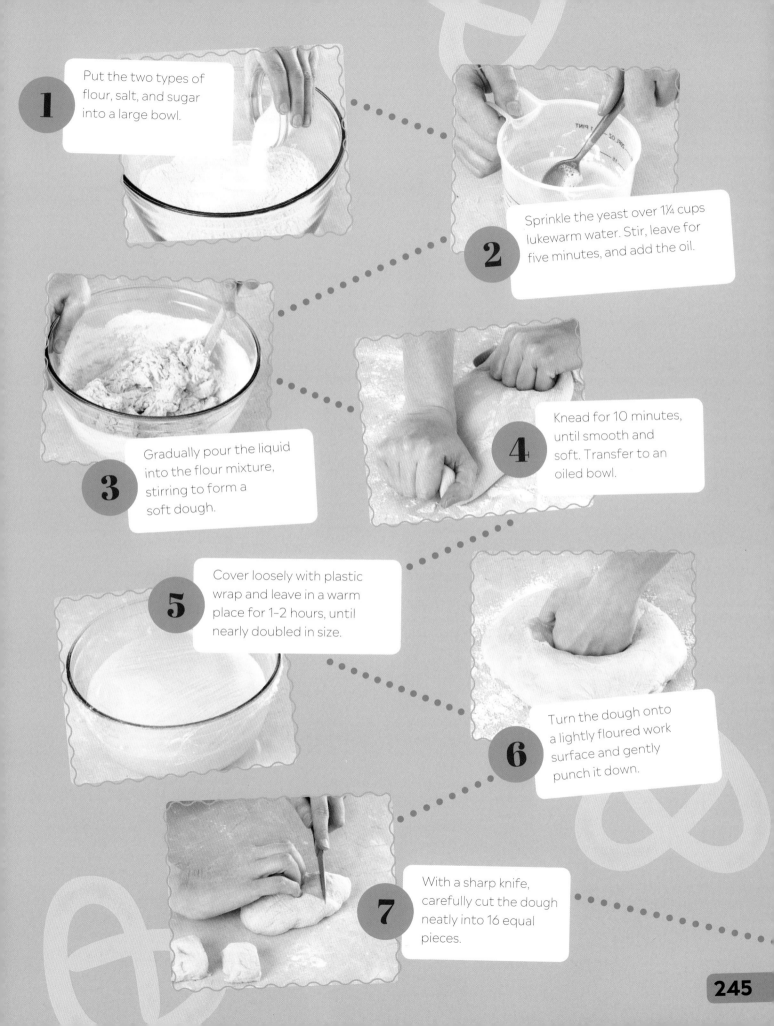

1. Put the two types of flour, salt, and sugar into a large bowl.

2. Sprinkle the yeast over 1¼ cups lukewarm water. Stir, leave for five minutes, and add the oil.

3. Gradually pour the liquid into the flour mixture, stirring to form a soft dough.

4. Knead for 10 minutes, until smooth and soft. Transfer to an oiled bowl.

5. Cover loosely with plastic wrap and leave in a warm place for 1–2 hours, until nearly doubled in size.

6. Turn the dough onto a lightly floured work surface and gently punch it down.

7. With a sharp knife, carefully cut the dough neatly into 16 equal pieces.

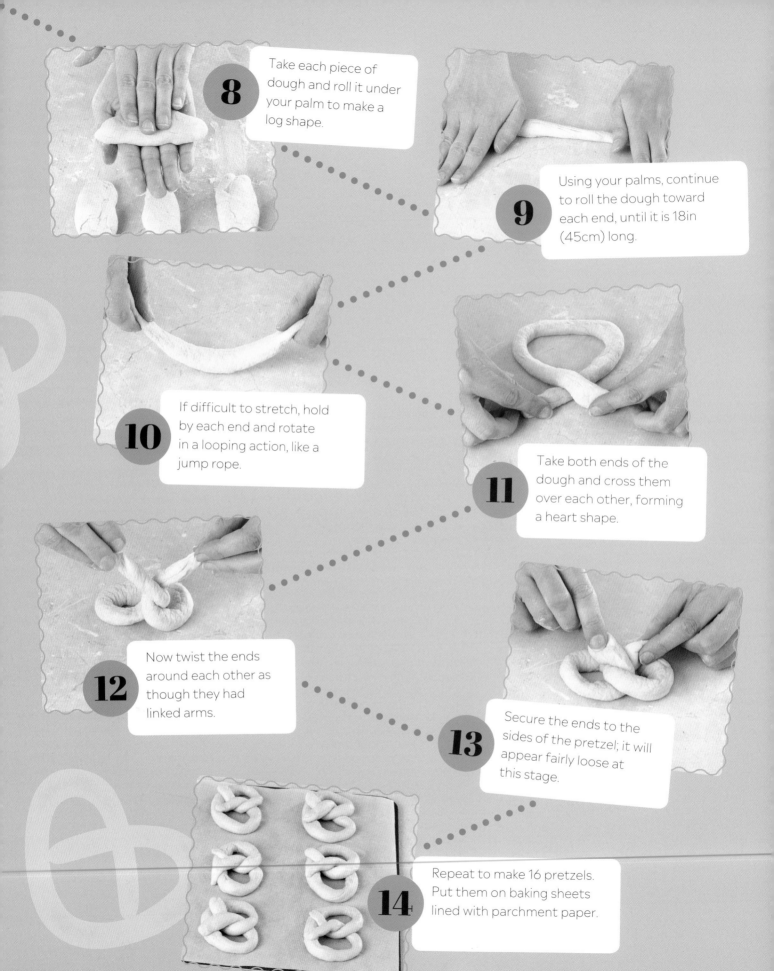

8 Take each piece of dough and roll it under your palm to make a log shape.

9 Using your palms, continue to roll the dough toward each end, until it is 18in (45cm) long.

10 If difficult to stretch, hold by each end and rotate in a looping action, like a jump rope.

11 Take both ends of the dough and cross them over each other, forming a heart shape.

12 Now twist the ends around each other as though they had linked arms.

13 Secure the ends to the sides of the pretzel; it will appear fairly loose at this stage.

14 Repeat to make 16 pretzels. Put them on baking sheets lined with parchment paper.

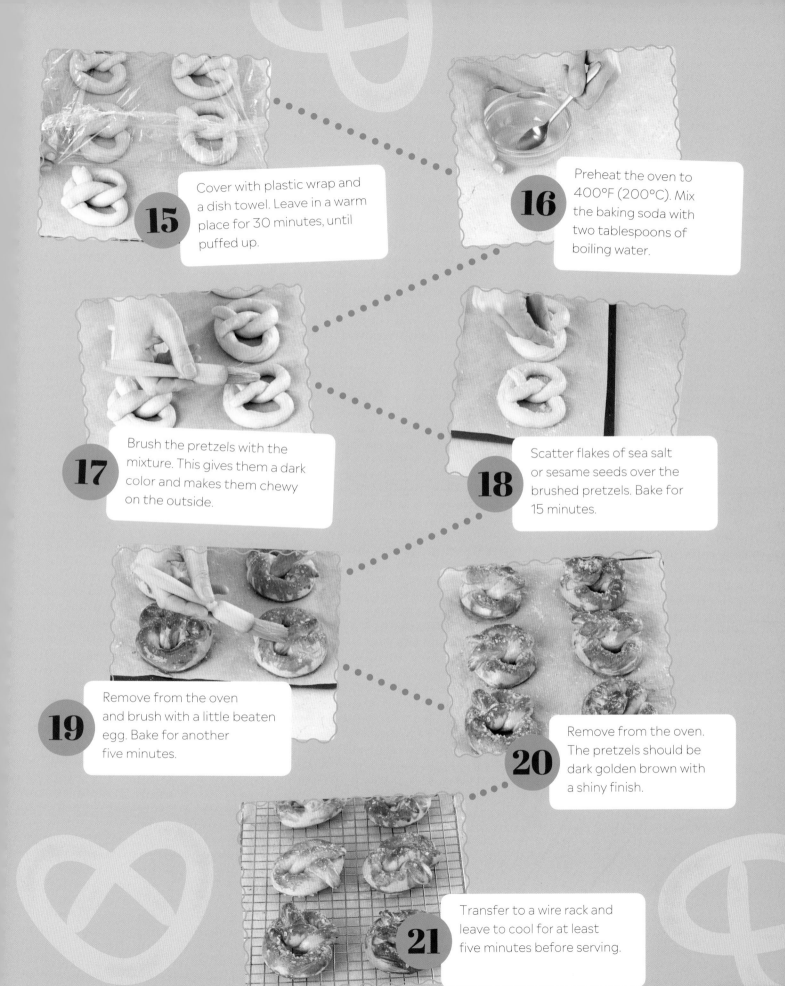

15 Cover with plastic wrap and a dish towel. Leave in a warm place for 30 minutes, until puffed up.

16 Preheat the oven to 400°F (200°C). Mix the baking soda with two tablespoons of boiling water.

17 Brush the pretzels with the mixture. This gives them a dark color and makes them chewy on the outside.

18 Scatter flakes of sea salt or sesame seeds over the brushed pretzels. Bake for 15 minutes.

19 Remove from the oven and brush with a little beaten egg. Bake for another five minutes.

20 Remove from the oven. The pretzels should be dark golden brown with a shiny finish.

21 Transfer to a wire rack and leave to cool for at least five minutes before serving.

Tear and share pesto bread

This homemade loaf is perfect for sharing at mealtimes and parties. Bring it out to "oohs" and "aahs" from your friends and family.

Level rating 🧁🧁🧁

How long? 45 mins prep,
2 hrs rising and proofing,
35 mins baking

How many? 1 loaf

Ingredients

2½ tsp dried yeast

¾ cup rye flour

1⅔ cups unbleached flour, plus extra for dusting

2 tsp salt

oil, for brushing

For the filling

⅔ cup green pesto

1 In a small bowl, dissolve the yeast in ¼ cup lukewarm water.

2 Mix the yeast, rye flour, 1¼ cups of the white flour, salt, and one cup lukewarm water in a large bowl. Add the rest of the white flour, ⅓ cup at a time. Mix until a smooth dough has formed.

3 On a floured surface, shape the dough into a ball. Put the dough in an oiled glass bowl, cover with plastic wrap, and leave in a warm place until doubled in size.

5 Spread the pesto over the dough, leaving a ½in (1cm) border. Use your hands to roll up the dough into a neat and tight cylinder.

4 Brush a baking sheet with oil. Knead the dough on a lightly floured surface. Cover with a dish towel and rest for five minutes. Roll the dough into a rectangle 16 x 12in (40 x 30cm).

7

Preheat the oven to 425°F (220°C).

6

Put the dough, seam-side down, on the baking sheet. Curve it into a ring and seal the ends. Make a series of deep cuts around the ring, about 2in (5cm) apart. Pull the sections apart slightly. Cover with a dish towel and leave to rise in a warm place for 45 minutes.

8

Brush the dough with oil. Bake for 10 minutes. Reduce the oven temperature to 375°F (190°C). Bake for another 20-25 minutes, until well browned. Cool on a wire rack.

SHARE AT A PARTY!

TRY THIS

Use red pesto instead of green for the filling in this bread.

Four seasons pizza

This tasty pizza has four different toppings all at once! You can prepare the sauce a day ahead and let the dough rise overnight, to quickly assemble the next day.

Level rating

How long?   40 mins prep,
1½ hrs rising,
20 mins baking

How many?   4

1 Mix the flour and salt. In a separate bowl, dissolve the yeast in 1½ cups tepid water. Add the oil to the yeast mix, then combine with the flour mix to form a dough.

2 Knead on a floured surface for 10 minutes, or until the dough is smooth and elastic.

3 Roll the dough into a ball and place in an oiled bowl. Cover with oiled plastic wrap. Leave in a warm place for 1–1½ hours, until doubled in size, or store in the fridge overnight.

4 For the sauce, put a pan over low heat. Add the butter, shallots, oil, bay leaf, and garlic. Stir and cover for 5–6 minutes, stirring occasionally.

Ingredients

2¾ cups bread flour, plus
    extra for dusting
½ tsp salt
3 tsp dried yeast
2 tbsp olive oil, plus extra for greasing

For the tomato sauce

2 tbsp unsalted butter
2 shallots, finely chopped
1 tbsp olive oil
1 bay leaf
3 garlic cloves, crushed
2¼lb (1kg) ripe plum tomatoes,
    seeded and chopped
2 tbsp tomato paste
1 tbsp granulated sugar
sea salt and freshly ground black pepper

For the toppings

6oz (175g) mozzarella, drained
    and thinly sliced
4oz (115g) mushrooms, thinly sliced
2 tbsp extra-virgin olive oil
2 roasted red bell peppers, thinly sliced
8 anchovy fillets, halved lengthwise
4oz (115g) pepperoni, thinly sliced
2 tbsp capers
8 artichoke hearts, halved
12 black olives

Special equipment

4 baking sheets or pizza pans

5 Add the tomatoes, paste, and sugar. Cook for five minutes, while stirring. Pour in one cup of water, bring to a boil, and reduce the heat to simmer.

6 Cook for 30 minutes, stirring, until it forms a thick sauce. Season with salt and pepper. Using a wooden spoon, press the sauce through a sieve. Cover and chill until needed.

7 Preheat the oven to 400°F (200°C). Put the dough on a floured surface. Knead lightly, divide into four, and roll or press out into 9in (23cm) rounds.

8 Grease the baking sheets and carefully lift the pizza crusts onto each sheet. Spread the sauce over the crusts, leaving a ¾in (2cm) border around the edges.

9 Top the pizzas with the mozzarella. Arrange the mushroom slices on a quarter of each pizza and brush with the olive oil.

10 Pile the roasted bell pepper slices on another quarter, with the anchovy fillets on top. Use pepperoni and capers for the third and artichokes and olives for the fourth quarter.

11 Bake, two at a time, for 15–20 minutes, or until the topping is golden and the crust is crispy. Serve hot.

Two ways
with pizza

Have a pizza party with these delicious pizzas! Bianca is covered in a creamy white sauce instead of tomato, and a calzone is a folded pizza with a tasty surprise inside.

Level rating

How long?
25 mins prep,
1½ hrs rising (Bianca),
2 hrs rising (Calzone),
20 mins baking

How many?
4

Pizza **bianca**

Ingredients

2¾ cups bread flour,
   plus extra for dusting
½ tsp salt
3 tsp dried yeast
2 tbsp olive oil, plus extra for greasing

For the topping
¼ cup extra-virgin olive oil
5oz (140g) Gorgonzola cheese, crumbled
12 slices prosciutto, torn into strips
4 fresh figs, each cut into 8 wedges
   and peeled
2 tomatoes, seeded and diced
4oz (115g) arugula
   freshly ground black pepper

1 To make the dough, follow Steps 1, 2, 3, and 7 on pages 250–251. Divide the dough into four portions. Preheat the oven to 400°F (200°C).

2 Brush the pizzas with half the olive oil and scatter the cheese over the top. Bake for 20 minutes, or until the crusts are crisp.

3 Remove from the oven. Arrange the prosciutto, figs, and tomatoes on top. Return to the oven for another eight minutes, or until the toppings are just warmed and the crusts are golden brown.

4 Scatter the arugula over the top, season with plenty of black pepper, and drizzle with the rest of the olive oil. Serve immediately.

Calzone

Ingredients

2¾ cups bread flour,
  plus extra for dusting
½ tsp salt
3 tsp dried yeast
2 tbsp olive oil, plus extra for greasing

For the filling
¼ cup extra-virgin olive oil,
  plus extra to serve
2 onions, thinly sliced
2 red bell peppers, cored and cut into strips
1 green bell pepper, cored and cut into strips
1 yellow bell pepper, cored and cut into strips
3 garlic cloves, finely chopped
1 small bunch of any herb, such as rosemary,
  thyme, basil, or parsley, or a mixture,
  finely chopped
sea salt
cayenne pepper, to taste
6oz (175g) mozzarella, drained and sliced
1 large egg, beaten, for glazing
½ tsp salt

1 To make the dough, follow Steps 1, 2, and 3 on page 250.

2 Heat one tablespoon of oil in a pan and add the onions. Cook for five minutes, until soft but not brown. Put in a bowl and set aside.

3 Add the remaining oil to the pan with the bell peppers, garlic, and herbs. Season with sea salt and cayenne pepper. Fry for 7–10 minutes, stirring, until soft but not brown. Add to the onions, then let the mixture cool.

4 Move the dough to a floured surface. Knead lightly, divide into four, and then roll and pull each piece into a square ½in (1cm) thick.

5 Spoon the bell pepper mixture onto a diagonal half of each square, leaving a 1in (2.5cm) border.

6 Put the mozzarella on top. Wet the edge of each square with water and fold one corner over to meet the other, forming a triangle. Pinch the edges together. Put on a floured baking sheet. Leave to rise in a warm place for 30 minutes.

7 Preheat the oven to 450°F (230°C). Whisk the egg with the salt and brush over the calzones. Bake for 15–20 minutes, until golden brown. Brush with a little olive oil before serving.

Pita bread

This pocket bread is delicious stuffed with salad and other fillings, or cut up and eaten with dips.

Level rating

How long?   30 mins prep,
1 hr 50 mins rising
and proofing,
5 mins baking

How many?   6

Ingredients

1 tsp dried yeast

⅓ cup whole-wheat bread flour

2 cups bread flour,
   plus extra for dusting

1 tsp salt

2 tsp cumin seeds

2 tsp olive oil, plus extra for greasing

1 In a bowl, mix the yeast with four tablespoons of lukewarm water. Leave for five minutes, then stir.

2 In a large bowl, mix together the two types of flour, salt, and cumin seeds. Make a well and pour in the yeast mix, ¾ cup lukewarm water, and oil.

3 Using a spoon, combine the ingredients to form a soft, sticky dough. Put on a floured surface.

4 Knead until smooth and elastic. Put the dough in a lightly greased bowl and cover with a damp dish towel. Leave to rise in a warm place for 1–1½ hours, until doubled in size.

5 Flour two baking sheets. Put the dough on a lightly floured surface and punch it down.

6 Shape the dough into a cylinder 2in (5cm) wide, then carefully cut into six equal pieces.

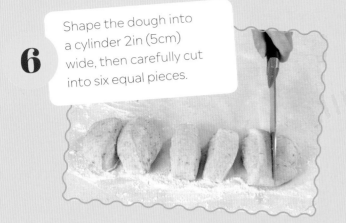

7 Take one piece of dough and leave the rest covered with a dish towel as you work. Shape the dough into a ball, then roll into a 7in (18cm) oval. Repeat with the remaining dough.

8 Transfer three pitas to a baking sheet. Cover with a dish towel. Leave in a warm place for 20 minutes and preheat the oven to 475°F (240°C).

9 Place the other baking sheet in the oven. Once hot, put the three pitas on the sheet and bake for five minutes.

10 Move to a wire rack and brush the tops lightly with water. Bake the remaining pitas, move to the rack, and brush with water. Let the bread cool before serving.

Naan bread

This traditional Indian flatbread goes perfectly with curry and is delicious when served warm.

How long?   20 mins prep, 1 hr rising,
8 mins baking,
1 min broiling

How many?   6

1 Heat the ghee or butter in a small saucepan until melted. Take off the heat.

Ingredients

4 tbsp ghee or unsalted butter

4 cups bread flour, plus
   extra for dusting

2 tsp dried yeast

1 tsp granulated sugar

1 tsp salt

2 tsp black onion (nigella) seeds

½ cup full-fat plain yogurt

2 In a large bowl, mix together the flour, yeast, sugar, salt, and onion seeds.

3 Make a well. Add ¾ cup lukewarm water, the yogurt, and the melted ghee or butter.

4 Fold in the flour and mix gently with a wooden spoon to combine.

5 Keep mixing for five minutes, until the mixture forms a rough dough.

6 Cover with plastic wrap and keep in a warm place for about one hour, until doubled in size. Preheat the oven to 475°F (240°C).

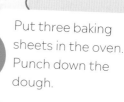

7 Put three baking sheets in the oven. Punch down the dough.

8 Knead the dough on a floured surface until smooth. Divide into six equal pieces.

9 Roll each piece into an oval shape about 10in (25cm) long. Remove the baking sheets from the oven.

TRY THIS
For garlic and cilantro naan, add 2 crushed garlic cloves and ¼ cup finely chopped cilantro in Step 2.

10 Put the bread on the preheated baking sheets and bake for 6–7 minutes until well puffed.

11 Preheat the broiler. Move the bread to the broiler pan.

12 Broil the naans for 30 seconds on each side, or until they brown and blister. Move to a wire rack.

Top tip
When broiling, make sure not to put the breads too close to the heat, to prevent burning.

Two ways with naan bread

Try stuffing simple naan bread dough with this herb-feta mix for a tasty picnic dish, or make peshwari naans for a sweeter flavor.

Level rating

How long?
15 mins prep,
1 hr rising,
6–7 mins baking

How many?
6

Feta, chili, and herb-stuffed naan bread

Ingredients

2¾ cups bread flour,
   plus extra for dusting
2 tsp dried yeast
1 tsp granulated sugar
1 tsp salt
2 tsp black onion (nigella) seeds
½ cup full-fat plain yogurt
4 tbsp ghee or butter, melted

For the filling
5½oz (150g) feta cheese, crumbled
1 tbsp finely chopped red chili
3 tbsp chopped mint
3 tbsp chopped cilantro

1 Mix the flour, yeast, sugar, salt, and onion seeds. Make a well. Add ¾ cup lukewarm water, the yogurt, and ghee or butter. Mix with a wooden spoon for five minutes to form a smooth dough. Cover and keep warm for one hour, until doubled in size.

2 Make the filling by mixing together the feta, chili, and herbs. Preheat the oven to 475°F (240°C) and put three baking sheets in the oven.

3 Divide the dough into six pieces and roll each one into a circle about 4in (10cm) wide. Split the filling into six portions and put a portion into the middle of each circle.

4 Pull the edges up around the filling to form a purse shape. Pinch the edges to seal. Turn the dough over and roll out into an oval, taking care not to tear it.

5 Put the naans onto the preheated baking sheets and bake for 6–7 minutes, or until well puffed. Move to a wire rack.

Peshwari naan bread

Ingredients

2¾ cups bread flour, plus extra
   for dusting
2 tsp dried yeast
1 tsp granulated sugar
1 tsp salt
2 tsp black onion (nigella) seeds
½ cup full-fat plain yogurt
4 tbsp ghee or butter, melted

For the filling

2 tbsp raisins
2 tbsp unsalted shelled pistachios
2 tbsp almonds
2 tbsp sweetened flaked coconut
1 tbsp granulated sugar

Special equipment

food processor with blade attachment

1 Mix together the flour, yeast, sugar, salt, and onion seeds. Make a well. Add ¾ cup lukewarm water, the yogurt, and ghee or butter. Mix with a wooden spoon for five minutes to form a smooth dough. Cover and keep warm for one hour, until doubled in size.

2 Make the stuffing by pulsing together all the ingredients in the food processor, until finely chopped. Preheat the oven to 475°F (240°C) and place three baking sheets in the oven.

3 Divide the dough into six pieces and roll each one into a circle about 4in (10cm) wide. Split the filling into six portions and put a portion into the middle of each circle.

4 Pull the edges up around the filling to form a purse shape. Pinch the edges together to seal. Turn the dough over and roll out into an oval, taking care not to tear it.

5 Put the naans on the preheated sheets and bake for 6–7 minutes, or until well puffed. Move to a wire rack.

Focaccia

This dimpled Italian flatbread can be flavored with herbs, cheese, tomatoes, or olives. Make it your own by adding your favorite ingredients to the dough.

Level rating

How long? 20 mins prep,
2 hrs rising,
25 mins baking

How many? 8

Ingredients

5 tbsp olive oil, reserve 1 tbsp for dipping,
   plus extra for greasing
2 cups bread flour
2 tsp dried yeast
1 tsp salt
sprigs of rosemary
sea salt, for sprinkling

Special equipment

11 x 7in (28 x 18cm) baking pan

1 Lightly oil the baking pan. Sift the flour into a large bowl and stir in the yeast and salt.

2 Make a well in the center and add one cup of lukewarm water and the oil. Mix until it forms a smooth dough.

3 Knead on a clean surface for 10 minutes, until smooth. Move to a clean bowl, cover with a dish towel, and leave to rise in a warm place for one hour.

4 Press the dough into the pan so it fills all the corners. Cover with plastic wrap. Leave to rise in a warm place for one hour.

5 Use your fingertips to make dimples in the dough. Sprinkle salt and scatter rosemary over the dough.

Drizzle OIL

6 Preheat the oven to 400°F (200°C). Bake for 20–25 minutes, until golden and crispy.

PACKED WITH
FLAVOR

Grissini sticks

This Italian breadstick is thin and crispy. It's simple to bake and perfect for a party or an afternoon snack.

Level rating 🧁🧁

How long?   45 mins prep,
                    1½ hrs rising,
                    18 mins baking

How many?   32

Ingredients

- 2½ tsp dried yeast
- 2¼ cups bread flour, plus extra for dusting
- 1 tbsp granulated sugar
- 2 tsp salt
- 2 tbsp extra-virgin olive oil
- 1½oz (45g) sesame seeds

1   Sprinkle the yeast over ¼ cup lukewarm water. Leave for five minutes, stirring once.

2   Put the flour, sugar, and salt in a bowl. Add the yeast and one cup lukewarm water.

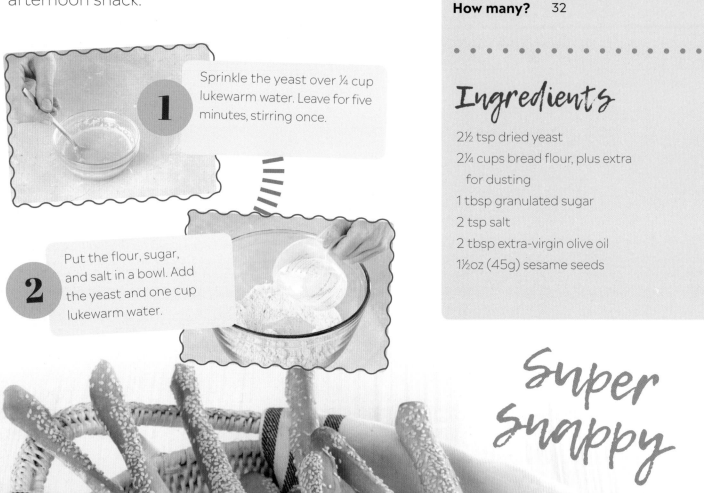

Super snappy

3 Add the oil and draw the flour into the liquid, mixing to form a soft, slightly sticky dough.

4 Knead the dough on a floured surface for 5–7 minutes, until very smooth and elastic.

5 Cover the dough with a damp dish towel and let it rest for about five minutes.

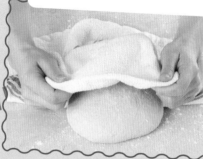

6 Flour your hands and pat the dough into a rectangle on a well floured work surface.

7 Roll the dough out to a 16 x 6in (40 x 15cm) rectangle. Cover it with a damp dish towel. Leave in a warm place for 1–1½ hours, until doubled in size.

8 Preheat the oven to 425°F (220°C). Dust three baking sheets with flour. Brush the dough with water. Sprinkle with sesame seeds.

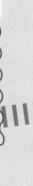

9 With a sharp knife, carefully cut the dough into 32 strips, each about ½in (1cm) wide.

10 Stretch the strips to the width of the baking sheets. Set them on the baking sheets, arranging them ¾in (2cm) apart. Bake for 15–18 minutes. Move to a wire rack to cool completely.

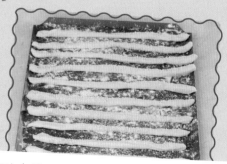

Onion and walnut crown

This delicious bread crown is packed with flavor!
It is ideal for lunch, served with your favorite cheese.

Level rating

How long? 30 mins prep,
2 hrs 15 mins rising and
proofing, 50 mins baking

How many? 1 loaf

Ingredients

2½ tsp dried yeast, dissolved in ¼ cup
   lukewarm milk

1¾ cups milk, plus extra for glazing

2 tbsp vegetable oil, plus extra
   for greasing

2 tsp salt

2¾ cups bread flour, plus extra for dusting

1 large onion, finely chopped

salt and freshly ground black pepper

2oz (60g) walnut pieces

1 Put the dissolved yeast, milk, one tablespoon of the oil, and the salt into a large bowl. Stir in half the flour and mix well with your hand. Add the remaining flour, mix well, and form into a ball. The dough should be soft and slightly sticky.

2 Knead the dough on a well floured surface for 5–7 minutes, until smooth and elastic. If the dough sticks while kneading, flour the work surface again.

3 Put the dough in a large bowl and cover with a damp dish towel. Leave it to rise in a warm place for 1–1½ hours, until doubled in size.

4 Preheat the oven to 350°F (180°C). Heat the remaining oil in a frying pan. Add the onion, salt, and pepper and fry for 5–7 minutes, until soft and light brown. Leave to cool.

5 Scatter the walnut pieces on a baking sheet and roast in the oven for 8–10 minutes, until lightly browned. Let the nuts cool, then coarsely chop them.

6 Grease a baking sheet with oil. On a lightly floured work surface, gently knead the dough to knock out the air. Knead the onion and walnuts into the dough until evenly mixed.

7 Shape the dough into a ball. Make a hole in the center of the ball with two fingers. With your fingers, make the hole bigger, turning to make an even ring, until the ring is 10–12in (25–30cm) in diameter.

8 Put the ring on the baking sheet. Cover with a dry dish towel and leave it to rise in a warm place for 45 minutes, or until doubled in size.

9 Preheat the oven to 400°F (200°C). Brush the ring with milk. Using kitchen scissors, carefully snip around the top of the ring in a zigzag design.

10 Bake the crown for 45–50 minutes, until well browned. Tap the bottom of the crown with your knuckles; the bread should sound hollow. Move to a wire rack to cool completely.

Perfect scones

These tasty scones, served with jam and cream or butter, will really hit the spot! The secret to making successful scones is not to handle the mixture too much and not to add too much flour when rolling out the dough.

Level rating

How long?   10 mins prep,
                  12 mins baking

How many?   8–10

Ingredients

4 tbsp unsalted butter, chilled
   and diced, plus extra for greasing
1½ cups self-rising flour, plus extra
   for dusting
1 tsp baking powder
pinch of salt
¼ cup granulated sugar
¾ cup milk
beaten egg or milk, for brushing

Special equipment

2½in (6cm) pastry cutter

1 Preheat the oven to 425°F (220°C). Lightly grease a large baking sheet with some butter. Sift the flour, baking powder, and salt into a large mixing bowl.

2 Using your fingertips, rub the butter into the flour mixture until it looks like bread crumbs. Stir in the sugar with a wooden spoon and mix well.

3 Stir in the milk with a butter knife to form a soft dough. Gently knead the dough on a floured surface to remove any cracks.

4 Roll out the dough to ¾in (2cm) thickness, then use the pastry cutter to cut into 8–10 circles. Gather up any trimmings, reroll them, and cut out more scones.

5 Put the scones on the baking sheet, spacing them a little apart. Using a pastry brush, brush the tops with the egg or milk and bake for 10–12 minutes, or until risen and golden brown.

6 Move the scones to a wire rack. Cut them in half and spread with butter and jam or with whipped cream and jam.

Cornbread

This tasty traditional skillet bread is super quick to make and goes well with soups and stews.

How long?   20 mins prep,
                25 mins baking

How many?   8

Ingredients

4 tbsp unsalted butter, melted and cooled,
    plus extra for greasing
2 fresh corncobs, about 7oz (200g)
    weight of kernels
1 cup fine yellow cornmeal or polenta
¾ cup bread flour
¼ cup granulated sugar
1 tbsp baking powder
1 tsp salt
2 large eggs
1 cup milk

Special equipment

9in (23cm) flameproof cast-iron frying
    pan or similar-sized loose-bottomed
    round cake pan

1 Preheat the oven to 425°F (220°C). Grease the pan with butter. Place in the oven.

2 Cut away the kernels from the cobs and scrape out the pulp with the back of the knife.

3 Sift the polenta, flour, sugar, baking powder, and salt into a bowl. Add the corn.

4 In a small bowl, whisk together the eggs, melted butter, and milk.

5 Pour three-quarters of the milk mixture into the flour mixture and stir.

6 Draw in the dry ingredients, adding the remaining milk mixture. Stir until smooth.

7 Carefully take the hot pan out of the oven and pour in the batter; it should sizzle.

8 Quickly brush the top with butter. Bake for 20–25 minutes.

Let the cornbread cool slightly on a wire rack.

9 The bread should shrink from the sides of the pan and a skewer should come out clean when the cornbread is done.

Top tip

Serve warm, with soup, chili con carne, or fried chicken. The cornbread does not keep well, but leftovers can be used as a stuffing for roast poultry.

Cinnamon rolls

These sweet rolls are packed with flavor. If you want to bake in time for breakfast, leave the rolls to proof overnight in the fridge (after Step 11).

Level rating

How long? 40 mins prep,
4 hrs rising and
proofing,
30 mins baking

How many? 10–12

Ingredients

½ cup milk

7 tbsp unsalted butter, plus extra
for greasing

2 tsp dried yeast

¼ cup granulated sugar

3 cups all-purpose flour, sifted, plus
extra for dusting

1 tsp salt

1 large egg, plus 2 large egg yolks

vegetable oil, for greasing

For the filling and glaze

3 tbsp ground cinnamon

½ cup light brown sugar

2 tbsp unsalted butter, melted

1 large egg, lightly beaten

¼ cup granulated sugar

Special equipment

12in (30cm) round springform cake pan

1 In a pan, heat ½ cup water, the milk, and butter until just melted. Let it cool to just warm. Whisk in the yeast and a tablespoon of the sugar. Cover for 10 minutes.

2 Put the flour, salt, and remaining sugar in a large bowl. Make a well in the center and pour in the warm milk mixture.

3 In a small bowl, whisk the egg and yolks, then add to the mixture. Combine to form a rough dough.

4 Put on a floured surface and knead for 10 minutes. Add extra flour if it is too sticky.

5 Put in an oiled bowl, cover with plastic wrap, and keep in a warm place for two hours, until well risen.

6 Prepare the filling by mixing two tablespoons of the cinnamon with the brown sugar.

7 When the dough has risen, turn it onto a floured work surface and gently punch it down. Roll it into a rectangle about 16 x 12in (40 x 30cm).

8 Brush with the melted butter and scatter with the filling. Leave a ½in (1cm) border on one side and brush it with the egg. Press the filling with your hand to stick it to the dough.

9 Roll the dough up, working toward the border. Do not roll too tightly.

10 Carefully cut into 10–12 equal pieces with a serrated knife, making sure not to squash the rolls. Grease and line the pan.

11 Pack in the rolls, cover with plastic wrap, and proof for 1–2 hours, until well risen. Preheat the oven to 350°F (180°C).

12 Brush with egg and bake for 25–30 minutes. Heat three tablespoons of water and two of sugar until dissolved. Brush over the rolls. Sprinkle a mixture of the remaining granulated sugar and cinnamon over the top, then turn onto a wire rack to cool.

BREAKFAST **TREAT**

Sticky fruit buns

Honey makes these sweet, fruity buns extra sticky! Traditional fruit buns are made with pumpkin pie spice, but you can leave it out if you like.

Level rating

How long? 25 mins prep,
2 hrs 10 mins rising,
30 mins baking

How many? 10

Ingredients

2¾ cups bread flour, plus extra
for dusting

¼oz (7g) package dried yeast

2 tbsp granulated sugar

1 large egg

17 tbsp butter, diced, plus extra
for greasing

¾ cup milk

For the topping

2 tbsp butter, melted

5½oz (150g) mixture of raisins, currants,
and golden raisins

1oz (25g) chopped mixed peel

⅓ cup light brown sugar

1 tsp pumpkin pie spice (optional)

grated zest of 1 lemon

1 tbsp honey

Special equipment

9in (23cm) round, shallow cake pan

1 Put the flour, yeast, and granulated sugar in a large mixing bowl. Make a well in the center and crack the egg into the well.

2 Melt the butter in a saucepan over low heat, then add the milk and warm through. Add this to the large bowl and bring together with a butter knife.

3 Turn the dough onto a lightly floured surface and knead for 10 minutes. Return to the bowl, cover with a clean, damp dish towel and leave in a warm place for 1½ hours.

4 Grease the bottom and sides of the pan and line the botom with parchment paper. Preheat the oven to 400°F (200°C).

5 Punch down the dough, then put it onto a floured surface. Roll the dough out to a 14in (30cm) square. Brush the melted butter all over it, using a pastry brush.

6 Mix together the dried fruit, mixed peel, sugar, spice (if using), and lemon zest. Sprinkle on the pastry, leaving a ½in (1cm) border. Gently roll up the dough into a sausage shape.

7 Use a sharp knife to carefully cut the dough into 10 pieces. Put them in the pan with their cut sides faceup. Cover them with a clean damp dish towel and leave in a warm place for 35–40 minutes.

8 Bake for 25–30 minutes, until golden. If they start to become too brown, cover them with foil.

9 Carefully brush the buns with the honey, taking care not to burn yourself on the hot pan. Leave the buns to cool in the pan for 3–4 minutes. Then turn them onto a wire rack.

FABULOUS AND FRUITY

Brioche des rois

Meaning, the "brioche of kings," in French, this bread is traditionally eaten at Epiphany, January 6. A trinket can be hidden inside to represent the gifts of the Three Kings.

Level rating

How long? 25 mins prep, 6 hrs rising and proofing, 30 mins baking

How many? 10–12

Ingredients

2½ tsp dried yeast

2 tbsp granulated sugar

5 large eggs, beaten

3 cups bread flour, plus extra for dusting

1½ tsp salt

vegetable oil, for greasing

12 tbsp unsalted butter, cubed and softened

For the topping

1 large egg, lightly beaten

1¾oz (50g) mixed candied fruit (orange and lemon zest, candied cherries, and angelica), chopped

2 tbsp coarse sugar crystals (optional)

Special equipment

porcelain or metal *fève* figurine (optional)

10in (25cm) ring mold (optional)

ramekin

1 Whisk the yeast, sugar, and two tablespoons lukewarm water. Leave for 10 minutes, then mix in the eggs.

2 In a large bowl, sift together the flour and salt.

3 Make a well in the flour and pour in the eggs and yeast mixture.

4 Use a fork and then your hands to bring everything together and form a sticky dough. Turn the dough onto a lightly floured work surface.

5 Knead the dough for 10 minutes, until elastic but still sticky. Put it in an oiled bowl and cover with plastic wrap. Leave to rise in a warm place for 2–3 hours.

6 Transfer to a lightly floured surface and gently punch down the dough.

7 Put one-third of the butter on the dough. Fold the dough over the butter and knead gently for five minutes. Repeat until all the butter is used up. Keep kneading until no streaks of butter show.

8 Form into a round and work it into a ring. Bury the *fève*, if using. Lightly oil a baking sheet and transfer the ring to the sheet or ring mold (if using).

Top tip

This bread will keep in an airtight container for up to three days.

9 Use a ramekin to keep the shape of the hole. Cover with plastic wrap and a dish towel. Leave to proof for 2–3 hours in a warm place, until doubled in size. Preheat the oven to 400°F (200°C).

10 Brush the brioche with beaten egg. Sprinkle over candied fruit and sugar crystals (if using). Bake for 25–30 minutes, until golden brown. Leave to cool slightly, then carefully turn onto a wire rack.

Hefezopf

This traditional sweet German bread is similar to brioche. Its simple braid is easier than it looks to achieve. It can be eaten on its own or with butter.

Level rating

How long?   20 mins prep,
4½ hrs rising
and proofing,
35 mins baking

How many?   1 loaf

Ingredients

2 tsp dried yeast

½ cup lukewarm milk

1 large egg

2½ cups all-purpose flour,
plus extra for dusting

¼ cup granulated sugar

¼ tsp fine salt

5 tbsp unsalted butter, melted

vegetable oil, for greasing

1 small egg, beaten, for glazing

1 Dissolve the yeast in the warm milk in a small bowl. Let it cool, then add the egg and beat well. In a large bowl, combine the flour, sugar, and salt. Make a well and pour in the milk mixture.

2 Add the melted butter and gradually draw in the flour, stirring to form a soft dough.

3 Knead for 10 minutes on a floured surface until smooth. Put the dough in an oiled bowl and cover with plastic wrap. Keep in a warm place for 2–2½ hours, until doubled in size.

4 Put the dough on a floured work surface and gently punch it down. Divide into three equal pieces.

5 Take each piece of dough and use your palm to roll it into a fat log shape. Continue to roll it toward each end until it is about 12in (30cm) long.

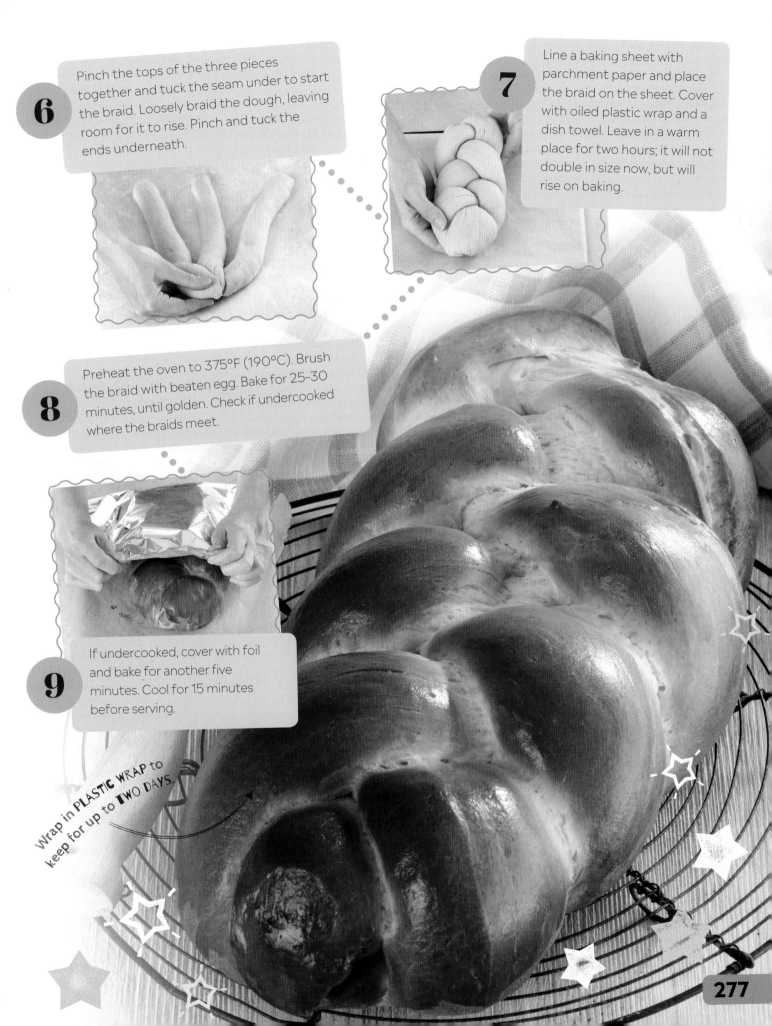

6 Pinch the tops of the three pieces together and tuck the seam under to start the braid. Loosely braid the dough, leaving room for it to rise. Pinch and tuck the ends underneath.

7 Line a baking sheet with parchment paper and place the braid on the sheet. Cover with oiled plastic wrap and a dish towel. Leave in a warm place for two hours; it will not double in size now, but will rise on baking.

8 Preheat the oven to 375°F (190°C). Brush the braid with beaten egg. Bake for 25–30 minutes, until golden. Check if undercooked where the braids meet.

9 If undercooked, cover with foil and bake for another five minutes. Cool for 15 minutes before serving.

Wrap in PLASTIC WRAP to keep for up to TWO DAYS.

277

Yule bread

This bread is a delicious festive treat. It needs to be baked a month before it's eaten, so that it can fully moisten and allow time for the flavors to blend.

Level rating

How long? 45 mins prep,
3 hrs rising and proofing,
50 mins baking

How many? 1 loaf

Ingredients

1 English breakfast teabag

3oz (90g) golden raisins

3oz (90g) currants

1½oz (45g) dried apricots, chopped

1½oz (45g) candied orange peel, chopped

3 cups unbleached white flour, plus extra for dusting

½ tsp ground cinnamon

½ tsp ground cloves

3 tbsp granulated sugar

1 tsp salt

2 large eggs

2½ tsp dried yeast, dissolved in ¼ cup lukewarm water

9 tbsp unsalted butter, softened and cubed, plus extra for greasing

2 tbsp brown sugar crystals, to glaze

Special equipment

1lb (450g) loaf pan

1 Soak the teabag in 1¼ cups boiling water for five minutes. Remove the teabag. Put the dried fruit in a bowl. Pour the tea over the fruit. Let the fruit soak in the tea for 15 minutes. Strain the fruit and reserve the tea.

2 In a large bowl, sift the flour, cinnamon, and cloves. Mix in the sugar, salt, reserved tea, eggs, and yeast. Use your hands to form it into a smooth dough.

3 On a floured surface, knead the dough for 5-7 minutes. Form it into a ball and put in a greased bowl. Cover with a dish towel and let it rise in a warm place for 1–1½ hours, until doubled in size.

4 On a lightly floured surface, knead the dough. Let it rest for five minutes. Knead in the butter for five minutes. Cover and let it rest for five more minutes. Knead the soaked fruit into the dough.

5 Cover and rest for five minutes. Grease the pan. Pat the dough into a rectangle 10 x 8in (25 x 20cm). Starting with a long side, roll the rectangle into a cylinder.

6 Roll the cylinder, stretching it until it is about 18in (45cm) long. With the cylinder seam-side up, fold the ends over to meet, making it the length of the pan. Put it in the pan, cover with a dish towel, and let it rise in a warm place for 45 minutes.

7 Preheat the oven to 400°F (200°C) Brush the top of the loaf with water and sprinkle the sugar crystals over the top.

8 Bake for 15 minutes. Reduce the oven temperature to 350°F (180°C) and bake for another 45-50 minutes. Remove from the pan and move to a wire rack to cool.

Top tip

To store the loaf, wrap it in parchment paper, then in foil, and keep it in an airtight container for a month before eating.

Panettone

This sweet bread is eaten throughout Italy at Christmas. Making one is not as hard as you might expect, and the result is delicious.

Level rating

How long? 30 mins prep,
4 hrs rising and proofing,
45 mins baking

How many? 8

Ingredients

2 tsp dried yeast

½ cup milk, warmed in a pan
   and left to cool to lukewarm

5 tbsp unsalted butter, melted

2 large eggs, plus 1 small egg,
   beaten, for brushing

1½ tsp vanilla extract

¼ cup granulated sugar

2 cups bread flour, plus extra for dusting

large pinch of salt

6oz (175g) mixed dried fruit, such as
   apricots, cranberries, golden raisins,
   and mixed peel

finely grated zest of 1 orange

vegetable oil, for greasing

confectioners' sugar, for dusting

Special equipment

6in (15cm) round springform cake pan
   or high-sided panettone pan

1 In a liquid measuring cup, add the yeast to the warm milk and leave for five minutes. Once the yeast mix is frothy, whisk in the butter, large eggs, and vanilla. In a large bowl, mix the sugar, flour, and salt.

2 Mix the liquid and dry ingredients to form a soft dough; it will be stickier than bread dough.

3 On a lightly floured surface, knead the dough for 10 minutes, until elastic. Form the dough into a loose ball.

4 Stretch the dough out flat onto a floured work surface. Scatter the dried fruit and orange zest on top and knead again until well combined.

5 Form the dough into a loose ball and put it in a lightly oiled bowl. Cover the bowl with a damp dish towel and leave to proof in a warm place for up to two hours, until doubled in size.

6 Line the pan with a double layer of parchment paper. If using a cake pan, form a collar with the paper, 2–4in (5–10cm) higher than the pan.

7 Punch down the dough with your fist and turn onto a lightly floured surface.

8 Knead the dough into a round ball just big enough to fit into the pan.

9 Put it into the pan, cover, and leave to proof in a warm place for another two hours, until doubled in size. Preheat the oven to 375°F (190°C).

10 Brush the top of the dough with the small egg. Bake for 40–45 minutes. If it is browning too fast, cover with foil. Leave to cool for five minutes, then turn out. Remove the parchment and cool.

Top tip

Dust with confectioners' sugar before serving.

NO-BAKES

No need to turn on the oven for these tasty treats. Simply crumble, melt, and stir your ingredients to make scrumptious snacks and delightful desserts. Then put them in the fridge until you're ready to enjoy.

No-bake cool cookies

Not all cookies need to be baked in the oven. These chewy cookies are so easy to make and use only a few simple ingredients. The peanut and chocolate flavor is really rich.

Level rating

How long?   20 mins prep,
30 mins chilling

How many?   12–14

Ingredients

¾ cup condensed milk

2 tbsp butter

2 tbsp light brown sugar

3 tbsp crunchy peanut butter

2 cups rolled oats

4½oz (125g) dark chocolate chips

For the filling

4½oz (125g) cream cheese

2 tbsp crunchy peanut butter

2 tbsp confectioners' sugar

1 Line two baking sheets with parchment paper. Put the milk, butter, sugar, and peanut butter in a saucepan over low heat. Stir until the sugar has dissolved and the butter has melted.

2 Take off the heat and stir in the oats until well combined. Let the mixture cool slightly, then stir in the chocolate chips.

3 Put rounded teaspoons of mixture on the baking sheets and flatten slightly. Chill for 30 minutes, until set.

CREAMY AND DREAMY

4

Put the cream cheese, peanut butter, and confectioners' sugar in a bowl and beat with a wooden spoon until smooth and creamy.

5

Spread a little of the filling on the flat side of a cookie, then sandwich together with another cookie. Repeat with the other cookies.

Top tip
The cookies will keep in an airtight container for up to three days.

Chocolatey no-bake bars

These crunchy chocolate, fruit, and nut bars couldn't be easier to make—they don't even need to be baked!

Ingredients

7oz (200g) bittersweet chocolate, broken into pieces

7 tbsp butter, diced

¼ cup golden syrup

8oz (225g) graham crackers, broken into pieces

4oz (125g) unsalted, shelled pistachios

7oz (200g) dried apricots, roughly chopped

3½oz (100g) dried cranberries or cherries

Special equipment

7 x 11in (18 x 28cm) pan

1 Line the bottom of the pan with parchment paper. Place the chocolate, butter, and golden syrup in a saucepan over low heat. Stir occasionally, until they are melted and smooth.

2 Place all the remaining ingredients in a large mixing bowl and mix well. Pour in the chocolate mixture and stir until all the ingredients are evenly coated.

3 Pour the mixture into the prepared pan and spread it out evenly with the back of a spoon. Chill for at least two hours, or until firm to the touch.

4 Run a blunt knife around the edge of the pan. Carefully turn onto a cutting board and remove the parchment paper. Cut into 18 squares and serve.

NUTTY AND CHEWY

TRY THIS

You can replace the dried cranberries or cherries with the same quantity of currants, raisins, candied cherries, or prunes.

Three ways
with no-bake bars

Try out these easy no-bake bars from around the world. Rocky Road was made in the US, Nanaimo came from a town in Canada, and Tiffin was invented in Scotland.

Nanaimo

Ingredients

Cookie layer
8 tbsp unsalted butter
¼ cup cocoa powder
¼ cup granulated sugar
1 large egg, beaten
7oz (200g) crushed cookies of choice
2½oz (75g) sliced almonds
1¾oz (50g) unsweetened flaked coconut

Vanilla layer
4 tbsp unsalted butter, softened
3 cups confectioners' sugar
2 tbsp custard powder
½ tsp vanilla extract
2–3 tbsp milk

Chocolate layer
5½oz (150g) dark chocolate, broken into pieces
2 tbsp unsalted butter

Special equipment
8in (20cm) square baking pan, greased and lined with parchment paper

1 Melt the butter in a saucepan and mix in the cocoa powder and sugar. Cook for two minutes, whisking continuously.

2 Reduce the heat and whisk in the egg. Cook for 1–2 minutes, until it has thickened. Remove from the heat.

3 In a large bowl, mix the cookies, almonds, and coconut together. Pour in the melted cocoa mixture. Combine well and transfer to the pan. Press the mixture down to make an even, firm layer. Chill for 30 minutes.

4 For the vanilla layer, beat the butter until fluffy. Add the confectioners' sugar, custard powder, vanilla, and milk. Beat until smooth. Pour it over the cookie layer and chill for another 30 minutes.

5 For the chocolate layer, melt the chocolate and butter in a heatproof bowl over a pan of simmering water. Cool to room temperature. Spread evenly over the vanilla layer. Chill for one hour.

6 Remove from the pan and slice into 16 even-sized pieces.

The CHOCOLATE will RIPPLE on top.

Rocky Road

Ingredients

9oz (250g) dark chocolate, broken into pieces
7 tbsp unsalted butter
2 tbsp golden syrup
5½oz (150g) pretzel sticks, roughly chopped
3½oz (100g) mini marshmallows
1¾oz (50g) unsalted almonds, roughly chopped
1¾oz (50g) dried cherries, roughly chopped

Special equipment

8in (20cm) square baking pan, greased and lined
  with parchment paper

TRY THIS
Instead of dried cherries,
you can try out raisins
or dried apricots in the
Rocky Road.

1 Melt the chocolate, butter, and golden syrup in a large heatproof bowl over a pan of simmering water. Cool to room temperature.

2 Add the pretzel sticks, mini marshmallows, almonds, and cherries to the chocolate mixture. Stir well until combined.

3 In the pan, spread the mixture out to a firm and even layer. Chill for at least two hours. Remove from the pan and slice into 16 even-sized pieces.

Tiffin

Ingredients

11 tbsp unsalted butter
½ cup golden syrup
⅓ cup cocoa powder
10oz (300g) graham crackers, crushed
5½oz (150g) dried fruit
9oz (250g) milk chocolate, broken into pieces

Special equipment

8in (20cm) square baking pan, greased
  and lined with parchment paper

1 Melt the butter, golden syrup, and cocoa in a saucepan over low heat, whisking constantly until smooth.

2 Combine the graham crackers and dried fruit in a large bowl. Pour over the butter mixture and mix together.

3 Pour the mixture into the pan and spread it out to a firm, even layer. Chill for at least 30 minutes.

4 Melt the chocolate in a heatproof bowl over a saucepan of simmering water. Cool to room temperature. Spread it over the cookie layer. Chill for 30 minutes.

5 Take out of the pan and slice into 25 even-sized pieces.

Top tip
All of these no-bake bars
can be stored in an airtight
container for up to five days.

Tasty tiramisu

This Italian treat is a light, layered dessert of coffee-flavored lady fingers and mascarpone that will melt in your mouth!

Top tip

This dish can be covered with plastic wrap and kept in the fridge for up to two days.

Level rating

How long? 30 mins prep, 6 hrs chilling

How many? 8

Ingredients

2 tbsp instant decaf espresso powder

½ cup almond syrup

For the filling

6 large egg yolks

1½ cups confectioners' sugar, sifted

⅓ cup vanilla syrup

1lb (450g) mascarpone cheese, at room temperature

2 cups heavy cream, chilled

14oz (400g) lady fingers

unsweetened cocoa powder, for dusting

Special equipment

13 x 9 x 2in (33 x 23 x 5cm) pan or dish

1 Measure out two cups boiled water and let it cool for five minutes. Mix the water with the espresso powder and almond syrup in a bowl. Set aside. For the filling, whisk the egg yolks and confectioners' sugar in a heatproof bowl for 2–3 minutes, until thick and pale in color.

2 Place the bowl over a saucepan of simmering water, making sure it does not touch the water. Add the vanilla syrup, whisking constantly to combine. Whisk the mixture for five minutes, until thick and ribbonlike in texture. Remove from the heat, cover, and cool.

3 Place the mascarpone in a large bowl and fold gently with a spatula to soften the cheese. Then add the cooled egg yolk and syrup mixture. Whisk gently until well combined and smooth.

4 In a separate bowl, whisk the heavy cream to form stiff peaks. Fold a little of the cream into the mascarpone mixture and mix well. Then gently fold in the rest and mix until it is well combined.

5 Dip half of the lady fingers into the coffee mixture, briefly, on each side, and use them to line the bottom of the serving dish. Cover with half of the cream filling and sift some cocoa powder over the top.

6 Add another layer of lady fingers and filling. Sprinkle generously with cocoa powder, wrap in plastic wrap, and chill for 4–6 hours. Remove the tiramisu from the fridge 15 minutes before serving.

No-bake lemon cheesecake

This zesty cold-set cheesecake doesn't need to be baked, making it lighter and fluffier than a baked cheesecake.

Ingredients

9oz (250g) graham crackers
7 tbsp unsalted butter, diced
1 tbsp unflavored powdered gelatine
finely grated zest and juice of 2 lemons
12oz (350g) cream cheese
¾ cup granulated sugar
1¼ cups heavy cream
pared lemon zest, to decorate

Special equipment

9in (23cm) round springform cake pan

1 Line the bottom of the pan with parchment paper. Put the crackers in a bag and crush into crumbs with a rolling pin.

2 Melt the butter and pour it over the crushed crackers, mixing well to combine.

3 Press the cracker mixture firmly into the bottom of the pan using a wooden spoon. Chill for 30 minutes.

4 In a small heatproof bowl, soak the gelatine in the lemon juice for five minutes to dissolve.

5 Place the bowl over a pan of hot water and stir until the gelatine melts fully. Set aside to cool.

6 Beat together the cream cheese, granulated sugar, and lemon zest until smooth.

7 In a separate bowl, whisk the heavy cream to form soft peaks. Make sure it is not stiff.

8 Beat the gelatine mixture into the cream cheese mixture, stirring well to combine.

9 Gently fold the whisked cream into the cheese mixture. Be careful not to lose any volume.

10 Pour the cheese mixture onto the chilled cracker crust and spread evenly.

11 Smooth the top with a damp palette knife or the back of a damp spoon.

12 Chill for at least four hours or overnight. Run a sharp, thin knife around the inside of the pan.

13 Gently turn the cheesecake onto a serving plate. Sprinkle the pared zest over the top. Remove the parchment paper before slicing.

Top tip
The cheesecake can be made up to two days ahead and stored in the fridge.

No-bake lime and blueberry cheesecake

This fruity cheesecake is packed with sweet blueberries and zingy limes, giving it a mouthwateringly good flavor. Make sure you measure the gelatine carefully to set the filling perfectly.

Level rating

How long?   30 mins prep,
                    6½ hrs chilling or overnight

How many?   8

Ingredients

9oz (250g) graham crackers,
   finely crushed
7 tbsp unsalted butter, melted

For the topping

3½oz (100g) blueberries
1 tbsp granulated sugar
grated zest of ½ lime

For the filling

juice of 2 limes
1 tbsp powdered gelatine
10oz (300g) sour cream
½ cup granulated sugar
1lb 2oz (500g) full-fat cream cheese
grated zest of 1 lime, plus extra to serve
1 tsp vanilla extract

Special equipment

9in (23cm) springform cake pan

---

1 Line the bottom of the pan with parchment paper. Combine the cracker crumbs and butter in a bowl. Spread the mixture in the bottom of the pan, pressing down firmly. Chill for 30 minutes.

2 For the topping, gently heat the blueberries, sugar, zest, and one tablespoon of water in a saucepan. Stir until the blueberries release their juices. Remove from the heat. Let cool.

3 For the filling, beat the lime juice and gelatine in a saucepan. Leave for five minutes. Then heat gently, beating, until the gelatine dissolves. Let it cool. In a bowl, beat the cream, sugar, cream cheese, zest, and vanilla, then beat in the gelatine mix. Spread the filling evenly over the graham cracker crust.

4 Spoon over the topping and decorate with the juices. Chill for 4–6 hours, or overnight. Take out of the pan and sprinkle with lime zest to serve.

Show it off

Once you've baked something special, you may want to show it off on social media, especially if it's the first time you've mastered a baking technique. Here are some tips on how to present and photograph everything from delicious pastries to pies, breads, and impressive celebration cakes.

1 Set the scene for your baked good. Would it be eaten at breakfast? If so, create a simple breakfast table setting. If you've made a showstopper cake for a party, then think about where it will sit. Could it be the centerpiece on a buffet table?

Top tip

Think about the timing. Does your baked good need to be shot right away, before it shrinks in size or melts? Does it need to be kept in the fridge until you're ready to whip it out to take a picture?

2 Select the right dish for presenting your baked good. Would a cake stand, plate, bowl, baking sheet, wire rack, wooden board, or basket work well? A tiered cake stand would be best for cupcakes, whereas a basket is perfect for bread.

3 Think about what the surface material should be. Would a tablecloth, patterned napkin, dish towel, or oven mitts add to the scene? Always choose simple patterns so you don't take the focus away from the food.

4 Choose the right dishware to be in the background of a shot, such as a pile of dessert plates or bowls. If it's a party scene, then perhaps paper plates or napkins in a stack would fit the mood.

5 Do you need any drinks in the background? Would a cup of tea, mug of hot chocolate, glass of milk or juice add to the shot? Make sure you select a drink that will go with the baked good you've made.

6 Would it help to have silverware, such as a sharp knife, cake fork, or cake slice to accompany your baked item? Try to keep it simple, and don't choose something that will take the attention away from the cake or other baked good.

7 Sprinkling a few extra ingredients around from the recipe can add to your photo. Use a small sieve to shake confectioners' sugar or cocoa powder over a baked good. You can also drop on edible glitter, sugar strands, or cake confetti. Scattered berries, edible flowers, nuts, and chocolate shavings can also add to the shot.

8 Adding in decorative elements, such as bunting, gift bags, balloons, and presents can really help enhance your photo. However, don't let the party bits and pieces take over the shot.

Snap and share

Taking a decent photo of food doesn't just happen by luck. You need to think about lighting, orientation, color, focus, shadows, angles, and backgrounds. These are skills you can easily learn when you're setting up something to snap on your camera or phone.

Think about...

TRY THIS

Flick through this book to get ideas. Which shots of the finished baked goods inspire you? Follow baking bloggers or vloggers. Read a few cooking magazines that specialize in baking.

Color
Make sure the surface color works for the food you're photographing. See pages 296–297 for advice on choosing props. Don't let strong patterns on a tablecloth take attention away from the food.

Shadows
If you take a photo outside then do so on a cloudy day. Bright sunshine casts strong shadows. A cloudy sky is better, since the light is more even.

Lighting
Natural daylight is ideal for taking photos of food. Artificial light can wash out the image and make the food look unappealing. Shoot inside and near a window.

Angle
Try out different angles. You can photograph your food overhead, straight on, or from an angle, looking slightly down or tilted up.

Orientation
Decide if a photo taken landscape or portrait would best showcase your finished work. For example, a tiered cake stand is tall, so might be better taken as a portrait shot. These pretzels work well in landscape.

Focus
Choose where you want your focal point to be. A lot of mobile phones and tablets allow you to click and pinpoint exactly where you want the camera to focus.

Background
Clear away any clutter, unless you want a messy shot of all the aftermath of baking a cake. Neutral wallpaper or a lightly painted wall both work well as backgrounds.

Overhead

This focaccia bread looks great when photographed overhead. The oil and balsamic vinegar dip also add to the setup of this final shot. It's irresistible!

Variations

Think about getting lots of variations. Always take a photo of the whole cake, for example, before you cut out a slice.

Less is more

Remember, it's the food you're trying to show off, so don't over-style or prop your picture. This impressive chocolate roulade has been placed on a white dish and plain tablecloth, to show off the food, not the props.

Adding in extras

Photograph a cake on its own, before adding in extras to create a different look. Place a relevant item from the recipe, such as this cut and partially peeled orange. Don't overdo it though.

How many?

Consider how many items you want to photograph. If you've made a batch of muffins, do you want one muffin in the foreground and the rest on a wire rack in the background?

Share it

Once you've taken the perfect picture, share it with your family and friends. They'll probably want the recipe, too.

Glossary

This is the place to find extra information about the baking terms and techniques used in this book.

A, B

alternate to take turns doing two things, such as adding an egg, then some sugar, then adding another egg.

baking blind weighing down a pie crust with baking beans or foil to stop it from rising during baking.

bar a sweet food that is made in a square or rectangular pan.

batch making or baking things a little at a time, usually if you do not have enough pans or space in the oven.

batter a thin, liquidy dough that is used to make light cakes, pancakes, and to coat food before it's fried.

beat stirring or mixing quickly until smooth, using a whisk, spoon, or electric mixer.

blend mixing ingredients together in a blender or food processor until combined.

boil heating liquid in a pan over high temperature so that it bubbles strongly.

C

chill cooling food in the refrigerator.

choux soft pastry that is piped onto a baking sheet instead of being rolled out. The dough bakes to form crisp, hollow balls that are then filled.

coarse food that is cut in small pieces.

combine mixing ingredients together evenly.

compote fruit cooked in syrup.

consistency how runny or thick a mixture is.

cream beating butter and sugar together to add air.

crème pâtissière a creamy custard used as a filling.

crimp shaping something into small ridges, or folds.

crumb coat thin layer of frosting applied to a cake to trap the crumbs, before a final layer of frosting is applied.

curdle when the liquid and solid parts of an ingredient or mixture separate. Milk curdles when overheated and cake mixtures can curdle if the eggs are too cold or added too quickly.

D

dice cutting an ingredient into small, equal cubes.

dissolve melting or liquifying a substance (often sugar in water).

dough the mixture of flour, water, sugar, salt, and yeast (and possibly other ingredients) before it is baked into bread.

drain removing excess liquid by pouring ingredients through a colander, or by resting on paper towels.

drizzle pouring slowly, in a trickle.

E, F, G, H

elastic a mixture with a stretchy texture.

fine incredibly small, often powdery pieces of food that have been ground down from a larger portion.

fold mixing ingredients together gently, to keep as much air in the mixture as possible.

fondant a thick topping that is rolled out, cut, and shaped into decorations for cakes, cupcakes, and pastries.

frangipane a paste made from almond-flavored cream and used as a filling.

frosting a topping that is usually a creamy icing.

fry cooking food in oil.

ganache a filling made from chocolate and cream.

glaze coating food in a liquid to give it a smooth, glossy surface.

grate shredding an ingredient into little pieces by rubbing it against a grater.

grease rubbing butter or oil onto a baking sheet or pan to stop food from sticking.

hollow something that is empty inside. Bread sounds hollow when baked.

I, J, K

incorporate blending together.

individual a single one, or enough for one person.

juice squeezing liquid out of a fruit or vegetable.

knead pressing and folding dough with your hands until it is smooth and stretchy. This distributes the yeast and helps it to rise.

L, M, N, O

level making the surface of something the same height.

line placing parchment paper or foil in a pan so that food won't stick .

lukewarm mildly warm.

macaron a small, round dessert made from two cookie halves with a cream filling.

mash crushing ingredients with a fork or masher.

melt heating a solid substance until it becomes a liquid.

meringue a light and airy dessert that's made from beaten egg whites and sugar and baked until crisp.

mix combining ingredients together, either by hand or with equipment.

moist something that is slightly wet.

no-bake a sweet dish that is chilled in the fridge instead of baked in the oven.

overwork if food is handled, beaten, or rolled out too many times then it doesn't work as well in a recipe.

P, Q, R

palmier a sweet pastry that's made in the shape of a palm leaf.

pastry a sweet or savory baked good made from flour, fat, and water.

pasty a small pie made with pastry that folds around vegetables, meat, or cheese.

pavlova a dessert made with a meringue bottom and filled with cream and fresh fruit.

peaks raised areas that look like the tops of mountains.

phyllo tissue-thin sheets of pastry. Best to use store-bought, as making it from scratch is incredibly difficult.

pie a baked pastry (savory or sweet) that usually has an outer crust and a top.

pipe making a strip of icing as a decoration on a cake or cupcake. Meringues are also piped from a piping bag.

pit removing the pit from fruit or vegetables.

portion an amount or helping of food.

preheat turning the oven on and heating it to the correct temperature before baking food in it.

process blending an ingredient or ingredients in a food processor.

proofing the final rise of bread dough before baking.

pulp mashing food so that it's crushed, wet, and soft.

punch down deflating risen dough with a gentle punch. This evens out the texture of the bread.

quantity how much of an ingredient you need.

rest putting pastry in a cool place.

rich strongly flavored.

ripe when a fruit is soft and ready to be eaten.

rise dough gets bigger in size when left in a warm place.

roll out flattening out and shaping dough or pastry using a rolling pin.

rub in rubbing flour and butter with your fingers to create a crumblike texture.

S

sandwich sticking two sides or halves together, usually with a mixture in between.

savory something that does not taste sweet.

score making small cuts across the top of a baked good.

season adding salt, pepper, vinegar, or other spices to a dish to add flavor.

serrated the pointed, toothlike edge of a knife.

set leaving food on the work surface, in the fridge, or in the freezer until it firms up and turns solid.

shortcrust pastry a crisp and crumbly pastry that's used for tarts, flans, and pies.

sift using a sieve to remove lumps from dry ingredients.

simmer cooking over low heat, so the liquid or food is bubbling gently but not boiling.

skewer a metal or wooden stick with a sharp end.

slice using a knife to cut food into strips.

sprinkle scattering a food lightly over another food.

streusel a crumbly filling or topping that is often flavored with cinnamon.

T, U, V

tart a pastry crust that has a savory or a sweet filling.

tepid mildly warm.

texture the way something feels, e.g., soft, smooth, or moist.

tiers layers of cake stacked on top of each other.

transfer moving something from one place to another.

trimmings leftover pieces of dough or pastry from cutting out.

turn onto taking out of a pan or baking sheet and carefully laying on a surface used for serving.

volume, adding increasing the size of a mixture, such as when beating egg whites.

W, X, Y, Z

well a dip made in flour in which to crack an egg or pour liquid into.

whisk evenly mixing ingredients together with a whisk.

yeast a type of fungus that when added to flour, water, sugar, and salt causes the mixture to rise.

zest the skin of a citrus fruit that has been grated with a grater or a zester.

Index

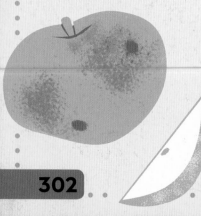

Acknowledgments

DORLING KINDERSLEY would like to thank the following people for their assistance in the preparation of this book: Dave King for photography, Anne Damerell for legal assistance, Laura Nickoll for proofreading, Eleanor Bates, Rachael Hare, Charlotte Milner, and Claire Patane for design assistance, Helen Peters for compiling the index, Anne Harnan for recipe testing, and Becky Walsh for hand modeling.

The publisher would like to thank the following for their kind permission to reproduce their photographs: (Key: a-above; b-below/bottom; c-center; f-far; l-left; r-right; t-top)
9 123RF.com: Lilyana Vynogradova (c). Dreamstime.com: Ra3rn (cla). 258 Dreamstime.com: Maglara (bl). 278 Dreamstime.com: Roberts Resnais (cla). 296 123RF.com: Belchonock (bl). 297 123RF.com: Serezniy (cra) **Cover images: Front: Alamy Stock Photo:** Tim Gainey, **Back: Alamy Stock Photo:** Tim Gainey

The publisher would also like to thank the following for their work on the original recipes that are re-used in this book:

The Cook's Book (ISBN 9780756613020)
Introduction: Jill Norman; Flavorings: Peter Gordon; Stocks & Soups/Poultry & Game Birds/Fruit & Nuts: Shaun Hill; Chinese Cooking: Ken Hom; Breads & Batters: Dan Lepard; Eggs & Dairy Produce/Pasta & Dumplings: Michael Romano; Fish & Shellfish/Vegetables: Charlie Trotter. Senior Project editors: Annelise Evans, Michael Fullalove, Pippa Rubinstein, Consulting editor Norma MacMillan, Senior Art editors: Susan Downing, with Alison Donovan, Editors: Lucy Heaver, Caroline Reed, Frank Ritter, Designer Alison Shackleton, Art director Carole Ash, Publishing director Mary-Clare Jerram, Publishing manager Gillian Roberts, DTP designer Sonia Charbonnier, Production controller Joanna Bull, Photographers: Steve Baxter, Martin Brigdale, Francesco Guillamet, Jeff Kauck, David Munns, William Reavell. Hugh Thompson, for his initial planning and management of the project. Bridget Sargeson, food stylist, for her unfailing professionalism and good humour in preparing and presenting for the camera over half of the techniques and recipes in this book. All of the chefs who generously made available their facilities and materials for photography. Editorial assistance Valerie Barrett, Shannon Beatty, Stuart Cooper, Roz Denny, Barbara Dixon, Anna Fischel, Kay Halsey, Karola Handwerker, Eleanor Holme, Katie John, Bridget Jones, Jenny Lane, Beverly le Blanc, Irene Lyford, Marie-Pierre Moine, Constance Novis, Gary Werner, Fiona Wild, Jeni Wright. Design assistance Maggie Aldred, Briony Chappell, Murdo Culver, Jo Grey, Toni Kay, Elly King, Luis Peral-Aranda, Judith Robertson, Liz Sephton, Penny Stock, Sue Storey, Ann Thompson. DTP design assistance Alistair Richardson, Louise Waller. Editorial consultation Rosie Adams, Henja Schneider, Margaret Thomason, Jill van Cleave, Kate Whiteman, Jennifer Williams. Index Dawn Butcher, Chefs' liaison Marc Cuspinera Viñas (for Ferran Adrià), Jennifer Fite (for Rick Bayless); Marion Franz (for Stephan Franz); Rosie Gayler (for Paul Gayler); Barbara Maher (for Stephan Franz); Anna Elena Pedron (for Norman Van Aken); Anne Roche-Noël (for Pierre Hermé); Lucy Rushbrooke (for Greg Malouf); Rochelle Smith (for Charlie Trotter); Elisabeth Takeuchi (for Hisayeuki Takeuchi); Jane Wareing (for Marcus Wareing); David Whitehouse (for Dan Lepard). On behalf of the contributing chefs prepared and styled food and demonstrated cooking techniques for photography: Sébastien Bauer (for Pierre Hermé), Jeffrey Brana (for Norman Van Aken), Marc Cuspinera Viñas (for Ferran Adrià), Julien Tessier (for David Thompson), Guiseppe Tentori (for Charlie Trotter). Food stylists Stephana Bottom, Angela Nilsen, Lucinda Rushbrooke (for Greg Malouf), Nicole Szabason, Linda Tubby, Kirsten West (for Rick Bayless), Sari Zernich (for Charlie Trotter). Susanna Tee for recipe testing. Hand models Virpi Davies, Harriet Eastwood, Saliha Fellache, Caroline Green, Jane Hornby, Olivia King, Emma McIntosh, Carlyn van Niekerk, Brittany Williams, Bethan Woodyatt, Tanongsak Yordwai (for David Thompson). Props stylists Victoria Allen, John Bentham, Bette Blau, Andrea Kuhn, Clara Farrell, Zoe Moore, Jolyon Rubinstein.

The Children's Baking Book (ISBN 9780756657888)
Recipes and Styling by Denise Smart, Photography by Howard Shooter, Project Editor Heather Scott, Senior Designer Lisa Sodeau, Editor Julia March, Home Economist Denise Smart, Managing Editor Catherine Saunders, Art Director Lisa Lanzarini, Publishing Manager Simon Beecroft, Category Publisher Alex Allan, Production Controller Nick Seston, Senior Production Editor Clare McLean, and US Editor Margaret Parrish.

The Illustrated Step by Step Cook (ISBN 9780756667535)
Editor Lucy Bannell, Project Editor Sarah Ruddick, US Editor John Searcy, Managing Editor Dawn Henderson, Managing Art Editors Christine Keilty, Marianne Markham, Senior Jacket Creative Nicola Powling, Senior Presentations Creative Caroline de Souza, Category Publisher Mary-Clare Jerram, Art Director Peter Luff, Production Editor Maria Elia, Production Controller Alice Holloway, Creative Technical Support Sonia Charbonnier, DK INDIA: Designer Devika Dwarkadas, Senior Editors Rukmini Kumar Chawla, Saloni Talwar Design Manager Romi Chakraborty, DTP Designers Dheeraj Arora, Manish Chandra, Nand Kishore, Arjinder Singh, Jagtar Singh, Pushpak Tyagi, DTP Manager Sunil Sharma, Production Manager Pankaj Sharma Photographers: David Murray, William Reavell, William Shaw, Jon Whitaker, Prop stylist: Liz Belton, Food stylists: Lizzie Harris, Sal Henley, Cara Hobday, Jane Lawrie, Phil Mundy, Jenny White, Art directors: Nicky Collings, Anne Fisher, Luis Peral, Indexer: Hilary Bird, Proofreader: Irene Lyford, Americanizers: Jenny Siklos, Rebecca Warren, and US consultant: Kara Zuaro.

Step-by-Step Baking (ISBN 9780756686796)
Author Caroline Bretherton Senior Editor Alastair Laing, Project Art Editor Kathryn Wilding, US Editor Rebecca Warren, Managing Editor Dawn Henderson, Managing Art Editor Christine Keilty, Senior Jacket Creative Nicola Powling, Senior Production Editor Maria Elia, Senior Production Controller Alice Holloway, Creative Technical Support Sonia Charbonnier, Photographers Howard Shooter, Michael Hart DK INDIA: Project Editor Charis Bhagianathan, Senior Art Editor, Neha Ahuja, Project Designer Divya PR, Assistant Art Editor Mansi Nagdev, Managing Editor Glenda Fernandes, Managing Art Editor Navidita Thapa, DTP Manager Sunil Sharma, Production, Manager Pankaj Sharma, DTP Operators Neeraj Bhatia, Sourabh Challariya, Arjinder Singh, Art Directors: Nicky Collings, Miranda Harvey, Luis Peral, Lisa Pettibone, Props Stylist Wei Tang, Food Stylists: Kate Blinman, Lauren Owen, Denise Smart, Home Economist Assistant Emily Jonzen, Baking equipment used in the step-by-step photography kindly donated by Lakeland, www.lakeland.co.uk, Caroline de Souza for art direction and setting the style of the videos and presentation stills photography, Dorothy Kikon for editorial assistance and Anamica Roy for design assistance, Jane Ellis for proofreading and Susan Bosanko for indexing. Thanks to the following people for their work on the US edition: Consultant Kate Curnes, Americanizers: Nichole Morford and Jenny Siklós, and Steve Crozier for retouching.

Get Started Baking (ISBN 9781465401953)
Senior Editor Alastair Laing, Project Art Editor Gemma Fletcher, Managing Editor Penny Warren, Managing Art Editor Alison Donovan, Senior Jacket Creative Nicola Powling, Jacket Design Assistant Rosie Levine, Pre-production Producer Sarah Isle, Producer Jen Lockwood, Art Directors Peter Luff, Jane Bull, Publisher Mary Ling, DK Publishing, North American Consultant Kate Curnes, Editor Margaret Parrish, Senior Editor Rebecca Warren, DK INDIA: Senior Editor Garima Sharma, Senior Art Editor Ivy Roy, Managing Editor Alka Thakur Hazarika, Deputy Managing Art Editor Priyabrata Roy Chowdhury, Tall Tree Ltd: Editor Emma Marriott, Designer Ben Ruocco, Written by Amanda Wright, Design assistance: Jessica Bentall, Vicky Kyte, DK Images: Claire Bowers,, Freddie Marriage, Emma Shepherd, Romaine Werblow, Indexer Chris Bernstein DK DELHI: Assistant Art Editor Karan Chaudhary, Art Editor Devan Das, Design assistance Ranjita Bhattacharji, Simran Kaur, Anchal Kaushal, Prashant Kumar, Tanya Mehrotra, Ankita Mukherjee, Anamica Roy, Editors: Kokila Manchanda, Arani Sinha, DTP Designers: Rajesh Singh Adhikari, Sourabh Chhallaria, Arjinder Singh, CTS/DTP Manager Sunil Sharma.

Step-by-Step Cake Decorating (ISBN 9781465414410)
Author Karen Sullivan, DK UK: Project Editor Martha Burley, Project Art Editor Kathryn Wilding, Managing Editor Dawn Henderson, Managing Art Editor Christine Keilty, Producer, Pre-Production Sarah Isle, Producers: David Appleyard, Jen Scothern, Art Director Peter Luff, Publisher Peggy Vance, Cake Decorators Asma Hassan, Sandra Monger, Amelia Nutting, DK US: US Senior Editor Rebecca Warren, US Editor Margaret Parrish, North American Consultant Kate Ramos, DK INDIA: Senior Editor Charis Bhagianathan, Senior Art Editors: Ira Sharma, Balwant Singh, Editor Janashree Singha, Assistant Art Editors: Tanya Mehrotra, Aastha Tiwari, Managing Editor Alicia Ingty, Managing Art Editor Navidita Thapa, Production Manager Pankaj Sharma, Pre-Production Manager Sunil Sharma, Senior DTP Designer Jagtar Singh, DTP Designers: Satish Chandra Gaur, Rajdeep Singh, Rajesh Singh, Sachin Singh, Anurag Trivedi, Manish Upreti.

Kids' Birthday Cakes Step by Step (ISBN 9781465421029)
Author Karen Sullivan, DK UK: Project Editor Harriet Yeomans, Managing Editor Dawn Henderson, Managing Art Editor Christine Keilty, Pre-Production Senior Producer, Tony Phipps, Senior Producer Jen Scothern, Art Director Peter Luff, Publisher Peggy Vance, US Consultant Kate Curnes Ramos, US Editor Jenny Siklos, US Senior Editor Margaret Parrish, Cake Decorators Sandra Monger, Hannah Wiltshire, Kasey Clarke, Juniper Cakery, DK INDIA: Project Editor Bushra Ahmed, Senior Art Editor Ira Sharma, Editor Ligi John, Art Editor Simran Kaur, Assistant Art Editor Sourabh Challariya, Managing Editor Alicia Ingty, Managing Art Editor Navidita Thapa, Pre-Production Manager Sunil Sharma, DTP Designers Rajdeep Singh, Manish Upreti, Mohammad Usman.

Desserts (ISBN 9781465438027)
Authors: Caroline Bretherton, Kristan Raines, DK LONDON: Project Editor Martha Burley, Senior Art Editor Sara Robin, Project Art Editor Vicky Read, Editorial Assistant Alice Kewellhampton, Design Assistant Laura Buscemi, Managing Editor Dawn Henderson, Managing Art Editor Christine Keilty, Senior Jacket Creative Nicola Powling, Pre-Production Producer Dragana Puvacic, Senior Producer Stephanie McConnell, Creative Technical Support Sonia Charbonnier, Deputy Art Director Maxine Pedliham, Publisher Peggy Vance, DK US: US Senior Editor Margaret Parrish, US Consultant Kate Ramos, DK INDIA Senior Art Editor Ira Sharma, Editors: Neha Samuel, Seetha Natesh, Art Editors: Zaurin Thoidingjam, Tashi Topgyal Laya, Deputy Managing Editor Bushra Ahmed, Managing Art Editor Navidita Thapa, Pre-production Manager Sunil Sharma, DTP Designer Rajdeep Singh.

Eat Your Greens (ISBN 9781465451521)
Senior Designer Sadie Thomas, Editors: James Mitchem, Carrie Love, US Editor Margaret Parrish, Editorial assistant Sopia Danielsson-Waters, Art direction for photography Charlotte Bull, Photographer Dave King, Food Stylist Georgie Besterman, Nutritional Consultant Fiona Hunter, Recipe Consultant Lorna Rhodes, US Consultant Kate Ramos, Senior Producer Leila Green, Pre-Production Producer Dragana Puvacic, Creative Technical Support Sonia Charbonnier, Managing Editor Penny Smith, Managing Art Editor Mabel Chan, Publisher Mary Ling, Art Director Jane Bull, Proofreader Caryn Jenner, Photoshoot Assistance: Eleanor Bates, Rachael Hare, Charlotte Milner, Illustrator Sadie Thomas, Picture Library Assistance: Lucy Claxton, Laura Evans. Models: Barney Allen, Lindsay Guzman, Egypt Hanson, Rio Lewis, Grace Merchant, Liberty Moore, and Olivia Phokou.

Cooking Step by Step (ISBN 9781465465689)
Senior Editor James Mitchem, Senior Designer Elaine Hewson, Art Direction for Photography Charlotte Bull, Designers: Charlotte Bull, Samantha Richiardi, Editorial Assistance Sally Beets, Carrie Love, Photographer Dave King, Home Economist and Food Stylist Denise Smart, Recipe Tester Sue Davie, Pre-Production Controller Tony Phipps, Senior Producer John Casey, Creative Technical Support Sonia Charbonnier, Managing Editor Penny Smith, Managing Art Editor Mabel Chan, Publisher Mary Ling, Art Director Jane Bull, James Tye for additional photography, Marie Lorimer for indexing, Eleanor Bates, Lynne Murray, Sakshi Saluja, and Romaine Werblow for picture library assistance, and Rachael Hare, Violet Peto, and Artie King for help during the photoshoots.